LOVE AND THE TURNING SEASONS

Translators

DEBEN BHATTACHARYA,

ROBERT BLY,

DILIP CHITRE,

ANANDA COOMARASWAMY,

VIDYA DEHEJIA,

HANK HEIFETZ AND V. NARAYANA RAO,

LINDA HESS AND SHUKDEO SINGH,

JANE HIRSHFIELD,

ARUN KOLATKAR,

DENISE LEVERTOV AND EDWARD C. DIMOCK JR.,

ARVIND KRISHNA MEHROTRA,

W.S. MERWIN AND J. MOUSSAIEFF MASSON,

LEONARD NATHAN AND CLINTON SEELY,

GIEVE PATEL,

EZRA POUND,

A.K. RAMANUJAN,

ANDREW SCHELLING,

GARY SNYDER,

CHASE TWICHELL AND TONY K. STEWART

LOVE
AND THE
TURNING SEASONS

India's Poetry of Spiritual & Erotic Longing

EDITED BY Andrew Schelling

COUNTERPOINT · CALIFORNIA

The Library of Congress has cataloged the hardcover as
follows:

Love and the turning seasons : India's poetry of spiritual &
erotic longing / edited by Andrew Schelling.
Includes bibliographical references.
ISBN 978-1-61902-241-6
1. Love poetry, Indic—Translations into English.
2. Erotic poetry, Indic—Translations into English.
3. Indic poetry—Translations into English. 4. Indic poetry
(English) I. Schelling, Andrew. II. Title: India's poetry of
spiritual & erotic longing. III. Title: India's poetry
of spiritual and erotic longing.
PK2978.E5L68 2014
891.4—dc23

2013028206

PB ISBN 978-1-61902-471-7

Cover design by David Bullen
Book Design by Gopa & Ted2, Inc

Counterpoint Press
Los Angeles and San Francisco, CA
www.counterpointpress.com

150870051

⦂ CONTENTS

Thou hast there in thy wrist a Sanskrit charge
To conjugate infinity's dim marge–
Anew. . . !
HART CRANE, *THE BRIDGE*

WE IN THE US inhabit a misplaced India, the land that Columbus thought he had found. Half a millennium later, the descendants of the original occupants are still bizarrely called Indians, no doubt because it has proven useful for the immigrants to treat the locals as foreigners. But if the story of Indian America is a huge and largely tragic epic, alongside it is a little anthology of lyrics, idiosyncratic moments: the invention of American Indias.

The mega-bestseller in the colonies, first published in 1751 and reprinted 54 times, was *The Economy of Human Life: Translated from an Indian Manuscript Written by an Ancient Brahmin*. This "ancient book" had been given by a lama in the Potala in Lhasa to a Chinese official named Caotsou, a man "of grave and noble aspect, of great eloquence," who translated it from the Sanskrit ("though, as he himself confesses, with an utter incapacity for reaching, in the Chinese language, the strength and sublimity of the original"). Translated from Chinese into English by an unknown hand, the book presented the "Oriental System of Morality" in a series of maxims on modesty, prudence, piety, and temperance, that seemed to emanate more from a Calvinist pulpit than the environs of an adorned lingam: "The first step to being wise is to know that thou are ignorant"; "The terrors of death are no terrors to the good'; "Take unto thyself a wife and become a faithful member of society"; "Keep the desires of thy heart within the bounds of moderation"; "Receive not a favor from the hand of the proud."

[The book, now believed to be the work of an English bibliophile named Robert Dodsley, had a curious afterlife. It was reprinted verbatim in 1925 by a group of California Rosicrucians as *Unto Thee I Grant,* the "Secret Wisdom of Tibet," which had been transmitted to the Himalayas by the pharaoh Amenhotep IV (Akhenaten– perennial occultist source of the world's religions). The text, in turn, became part of the ultra-secret *Circle 7 Koran* of the inner-city Moorish Science Temple, founded in Newark in 1913 by the prophet Noble Drew Ali (born Timothy Drew) and relocated to Chicago in the 1920's. Among the initiates of the *Circle 7 Koran* were Wallace Fard and Elijah Muhammad, who adapted the sacred knowledge to create the Nation of Islam. There is a line, then, however jagged, from pseudo-Hinduism to Malcolm X.]

Actual artifacts from India began to arrive in New England with the opening of the India trade in 1784: muslins, Bengal ginghams and paisley shawls, monkeys and parrots, tamarind and ginger, knicknacks and small statues of the uncanny gods. The first real Indian– a Tamil from Madras, with a "soft countenance" but "well-proportioned body"– showed up in 1790; six years later, the first elephant, named Old Bet, was a sensation. The East Marine Society, made up of sailors who had been to Asia, had a spectacular annual parade in Salem, with a "palanquin borne by Negroes dressed in the Indian manner."

Intellectual Indophilia begins with both global trade and Sir William Jones' discovery of the Indo-European roots of many languages, the realization that those strange others were somehow part of "us." Samuel Adams, in his retirement devouring books on the East, wrote to Jefferson that "Indeed Newton himself, appears to have discovered nothing that was not known to the Ancient Indians. He has only furnished more ample demonstrations of the doctrines they taught." Post-Revolutionary America's belief in (if not practice of) universal human rights was leading to a preoccupation with a universal human religion. One of the responses was Unitarianism, which found a bridge between the seemingly dissimilar Hinduism and Christianity in the figure of Rammohun Roy, who translated some of the Vedas and the Upanishads and founded the Brahmo Samaj, devoted to recuperating an imagined monotheistic ur-Hinduism, sweeping away the million gods. When Roy moved to London and converted to Christianity (or more exactly, the universal Hindu-Christianity) he became a Unitarian star.

Roy was read by Emerson, who said that India "makes Europe appear the land of trifles." In the Vedas, the *Bhagavad-Gita*, and the *Vishnu Purana*, he found the "highest expression" of the "conception of the fundamental Unity." His philosophical terms, the Over-Soul and the Higher Self, are plainly derived from the Hindu *Brahman* and *atman;* his versions of "illusion" and "fate" come from *maya* and *karma*. Curiously, though his beloved aunt sent him Sanskrit poems and he himself extensively adapted poems by Hafiz, Saadi, and other Persian and Arabic poets, Indian poetry didn't enter into his Indo-worldview and India only appears twice in his poetry: a lament for dead New England farmers, mysteriously titled "Hamatreya," (a word otherwise unknown, though possibly derived from Maitreya, the future Buddha, which doesn't illuminate the poem) and the often-anthologized "Brahma" ("If the red slayer think he slays, / Or if the slain think he is slain, / They know not well the subtle ways/ I keep, and pass, and turn again."), a poem that eerily seems indeed to come from the future: the voice of another Indophile, Yeats.

Thoreau discovered India through Emerson, and surpassed him in unqualified enthusiasm: "I cannot read a sentence in the book of the Hindoos [probably either the *Laws of Manu* or the *Bhagavad-Gita*] without being elevated as upon the table-land of the Ghauts. It has such a rhythm as the winds of the desert, such a tide as the Ganges, and seems as superior to criticism as the Himmaleh Mounts." He took the *Gita* with him to Walden and declared himself a yogi. (Some have seen his retreat to the pond as an act of yogic austerity, though his sisters often brought him cookies.) He was given a large library of Indian books, for which, typically, he built a special bookcase out of driftwood, and translated from the French some Buddhist texts and a story from the *Mahabharata*. But he was apparently untempted by the poetry, though he said that Indian "philosophy and poesy seem to me superior to, if not transcending greatly, all others." His enduring contribution to the Indo-American loop is, of course, his "civil disobedience," which inspired Gandhi's *satyagraha*, which inspired Martin Luther King's non-violent resistance.

Though Emerson called *Leaves of Grass* "a remarkable mixture of the Bhagvat Ghita and the *New York Herald*," though many critics have presented Vedantist readings of Whitman, it is likely that his actual knowledge of India was limited to a few magazine articles. Things Indian are scattered through the work, but merely as items in his human catalog; the "Hindu" aspects probably derive from intuition or experience or Emerson. "Passage to India," beyond its famously recycled title, is a celebration of the opening of the Suez canal as a metaphor for the joining of the Old and New Worlds, the past and present, and– "Passage to more than India!"– for the soul's voyage into the ether. Apart from a few lines in the sixth section, India itself barely appears, though the invocation of the "tender and junior Buddha" is irresistible.

Two years later, in 1893, the World Parliament of Religions in Chicago, dedicated to the dream of a single world religion in the new century, featured the glamorous Swami Vivekananda, the first Indian pop star guru, who, like the Brahmo Samaj, preached a Hinduism without gods: the Emersonian uniting of a human soul with the universal consciousness of a universal god. In the wake of his extensive speaking tours and the proliferation of branches of his Vedanta Society, the tabloids were full of stories of respectable Christian housewives suddenly abandoning hearth and home for a life of depravity. The dream of unity, from Vivekananda and the gurus who followed his trail, provoked its nightmare: the Immigration Act of 1917, which prohibited immigration to the U.S. by all Asians except Christian Fillipinos, and which remained in place until 1965.

In 1896, Mark Twain was the first American writer of note to actually make the passage to India, spending three months there on his around-the-world tour:

> This is India! The land of dreams and romance, of fabulous wealth and fabulous poverty, of splendor and rags, of palaces and hovels, of famine and pestilence, of genii and giants and Aladdin lamps, of tigers and elephants, the cobra and the jungle, the country of a hundred nations and a hundred tongues, of a thousand religions and two million gods, cradle of the human race, birthplace of human speech, mother of history, grandmother of legend, great-grandmother of tradition, whose yesterdays bear date with the mouldering antiquities of the rest of the nations—the one sole country under the sun that is endowed with an imperishable interest for alien persons, for lettered and ignorant, wise and fool, rich and poor, bond and free, the one land that all men desire to see, and having seen once, by even a glimpse, would not give that glimpse for all the shows of all the rest of the globe combined.

He wrote that "They are much the most interesting people in the world—and the nearest to being incomprehensible." The Indo-American century ends with his wisecrack: "East is East and West is West, and finally the Twain have met."

Anglo-American modernism exuberantly rummaged through the history of poetry– the Greek anthology, the Tang Dynasty, troubadours and Anglo-Saxon bards, the Metaphysicals, the haiku masters– but oddly never discovered classical Indian lyricism. Eliot's Sanskrit studies at Harvard led only to the famous last line of "The Waste

Land." Yeats translated ten of the Upanishads with Shree Purohit Swami, and dreamed that a modern poet would be inspired to create "some new Upanishad, some new half-Asiatic masterpiece," but apparently was unaware of the non-canonical texts. Pound collaborated with a young man named Kali Mohan Ghose– a member of the London branch of the Brahmo Samaj, whom he met through Rabindranath Tagore– and translated a few poems by Kabir, which were published in a Calcutta magazine in 1913. But other than a walk-on in the *Pisan Cantos*, Pound never mentioned Kabir again, nor did he translate or write about other classical Indian poets.

The "invention of China" transformed Anglo-American poetry, but nothing similar happened with India, despite the Indian currents floating around modern poetry. Pound practiced yogic breathing and was a life-long admirer of the writings of Yogi Ramacharaka (whom he did not know was actually William Walker Atkinson, born in Baltimore), where, among other things, he discovered the vortex that became Vorticism. Madame Blavatsky and Henry Steel Olcott were dead, but the Theosophical Society was not only promoting its quirky mythologies, but also serious scholarship in Hinduism and Buddhism. Theosophy was inescapable, and its ideas were not only known in varying degrees to the poets, they also colored nearly all the writing, scholarly or occult, on Indian religions and philosophies in the first half of the century. (Its creative masterpiece was the invention of the *Tibetan Book of the Dead*.) The great art historian and aesthetician Ananda Coomaraswamy had spurred interest in classical Indian art, and Tagore– friend of Yeats and Pound and everyone else– was an international phenomenon, easily the most famous poet in the world.

Yet taste and happenstance worked against Indian poetry. The texts that were widely known– mainly the canonical religious works and Tagore– had no place in the prevailing Imagist aesthetic against rhetoric and abstraction. (In Spanish, however, the young Neruda could plagiarize Tagore with no apparent stylistic rupture.) Nor was there in Sanskrit a figure who could occupy a place similar to that of Arthur Waley in classical Chinese and Japanese: that is, a reputable scholar who was connected to the contemporary literary life and capable of writing translations of interest to non-specialists. (Neither did India have a popular, literary, all-purpose, Western "explainer," as Japan did with Lafcadio Hearn.) And, if the religious-erotic *bhakti* poems presented in this anthology were known at all to the poets, it is doubtful they would have done much with them, for the Anglo-American poets, at least on the page, were a prudish bunch, compared to the novelists. Their poetry had no Lady Chatterleys or Molly Blooms; Hemingway's earth did not move. It would be hilarious to imagine Krishna and the *gopis* disporting in Eliot's East Coker or H.D.'s Delphi or Stevens' ordinary evening in New Haven or especially in Robert Frost's snowy woods.

Probably the first significant American poem located in India is Muriel Rukeyser's five-part "Ajanta," included in her 1944 *Beast in View*. Though presented as a "journey" from the first line ("Came in my full youth to the midnight cave"), Rukeyser had never been to India. Five years later, in the prose meditation *The Life of Poetry,* she has a few pages on Ajanta as a metaphor for poetry: "The sensation of space within ourselves is the analogy by which the world is known."

James Laughlin, the publisher of New Directions, spent two years in India in the early 1950s with the Ford Foundation, advising the new, post-colonial publishers. His verse-memoir *Byways* has an entertaining chapter set in Trivandrum, and his time there led to the publication of many classical and contemporary Indian and India-related books by New Directions, but none of them were lyric poetry.

The one major Indo-American poetry "event" or nexus in the second half of the 20th century was the fourteen months Allen Ginsberg and Peter Orlovsky spent traveling in India in 1962 and 1963, joined for part of the time by Gary Snyder and Joanne Kyger, and the mysterious Hope Savage, all in flight from Cold War USA. This "first encounter" (in the anthropological sense) of American poets and actual India is documented in Ginsberg's journals— one of the masterpieces of Beat prose— Snyder's quite beautiful journal, Kyger's more straightforward journal, and in a brilliant retelling by Deborah Baker, *The Blue Hand*. Ginsberg's involvement with the religious street singers, the Bauls, led to a few translations, and to recordings and tours in the US. Above all, passages in Ginsberg's journals and the uncharacteristically few poems he wrote in India come close to an American *bhakti*: the infinite sights, smells, sounds of India pour through in Whitmanian catalogs, all of them ultimately hallucinatory– sometimes literally drug-induced— and illusory. The only poet to carry on this tradition has been Anne Waldman, herself a later visitor to India.

It is surprising, as in the first half of the century, that the vogue for Indian things barely carried into poetry. Hippie travelers in Rishikesh or Benares, the Beatles, Ravi Shankar, the invocation of Gandhi in the antiwar movement, Hare Krishnas in the airports, Ginsberg's harmonium and chanting at his countless readings, the popularity of yoga and the parade of mass-market gurus. . . Yet there were only three noteworthy books by American poets, all slim: Denise Levertov's collaboration with Edward C. Dimock on Bengali songs, *In Praise of Krishna* (1967); Robert Bly's *The Kabir Book* (1976), a rewriting of Tagore's translations; and W. S. Merwin's collaboration with J. Moussaieff Masson (later Jeffrey Masson of the Freud archive controversy), *Sanskrit Love Poetry* (1977, reprinted as *The Peacock's Egg*). A. K. Ramanujan, who lived much of his life in the US, had the Tamil poems of *The Interior Landscape* (1967) and one book that was popular among poets: the Penguin *Speaking of Śiva* (1973), translations from the classical Kannada. Ramanujan was perhaps the closest to an Arthur Waley as both a literary figure and a scholar but, although revered in India, he was not widely known in the US. Among the Indologists, Barbara Stoler Miller, who died young, had a good translation of Bhartrihari (1967), and later of the *Gita*, and Daniel H. H.

Ingalls' massive *An Anthology of Sanskrit Court Poetry* (1965) remains an inexhaustible delight. Among India-inspired American poems, the most memorable are Charles Olson's "Poem 143. The Festival Aspect" in the third volume of *The Maximus Poems* (written in 1965), which came out of his reading of Heinrich Zimmer's *Myths and Symbols in Indian Art and Civilization*, and– with Ginsberg, perhaps the greatest example of an American *bhakti* of transcendent erotic lyrics– Kenneth Rexroth's *The Love Poems of Marichiko* (1978), which purports to be a translation of a contemporary Japanese woman poet.

Since then, the landscape has grown even sparser: some translations by the Indian poets Dilip Chitre, Arun Kolatkar, and especially Arvind Krishna Mehrotra; versions of Mirabai by Robert Bly and Jane Hirshfeld, a few scholars (most notably David Shulman, an immensely prolific translator of classical Tamil and Telugu). The editor of this anthology, Andrew Schelling, is the first American poet to translate directly from the Sanskrit. Incredibly, given the long history and oceanic vastness of classical Indian poetry, for some thirty years he has been virtually alone in the field.

This anthology gathers much of the best that has been done to date. It usefully serves one function of an anthology, as an introduction to a certain kind of poetry, written in certain languages in certain eras. But beyond literary history, beyond the many pleasures of the individual poems, it also serves the function of translation at its best– that is, as inspiration. Here is a poetry that does not exist in our language, but, transformed, it could.

ELIOT WEINBERGER

: Note on Translation and Pronunciation

W HEN ALEXANDER reached the banks of the Indus River in 326 BCE he encountered "the speaking tree." Human and animal figures hung from its trunk and branches, babbling in many or maybe all languages. The oracle-tree could answer questions in the tongue of "anyone who addressed it."

The 2001 census of India identified 1,600 different "mother tongues." In 2009 the census listed 452 "official languages," and speakers of nonofficial languages continue to petition the courts for recognition. Thirty of India's languages have more than a million speakers. This means that many, many languages may have had fine singers, but no accomplished translator has worked with the songs. I have drawn on translations done into English by Indian and American writers, most of them poets. It turns out that everything in this collection originates in one of those thirty languages spoken by big populations, except for a few instances where a vernacular such as Braj Bhaṣa is no longer used.

Most of India's languages fall into two families, Indo-Aryan and Dravidian. No matter how closely related, from region to region they pronounce words a bit differently. A few contain sounds borrowed from Persian or Chinese. Meanwhile, publishers and scholars have never fully agreed how to spell words when using Roman script. You can find books with the god written Shiva, Śiva, or Siva. The Rajasthani singer shows up as Mira, Mīra, or Meera.

Some of the translators in this volume use diacritical marks, others skip them: rāga or raga. I have followed the way each chose to spell names and words, out of respect for their individual decisions, though it makes this book look inconsistent.

For the commentaries I've spelled familiar names and places the way you'd see them in a newspaper: Rajasthan and Varanasi, Mirabai and Ramanujan. Less familiar words and names I tend to give with diacritical marks to help with pronunciation.

Vowels sound like this (some differences region to region):

a	as in *hut*
ā	as in *fa*ther
i	as in *hit*
ī	as in *heat*
u	as in *put*
ū	as in *boot*
ṛ (or ri)	as in *cri*cket (with a little flap of the tongue against the roof of the mouth)
e	as in *say*
ai	as in *aisle*
o	as in *poke*
au	as in *cow*

Consonants sound pretty much as in English, though the *c* is a *ch* sound. Note that after a consonant an *h* signifies a tiny outbreath that does not change the quality of the vowel. *Th* is a *t* followed by a tiny outbreath, *top*; similarly, *ph* sounds like the *p* in *pot*.

You might not notice the difference between these:

ś	as in *shut* (soft palate)
ṣ	as in *harsh* (hard palate)

: Translators

DB	Deben Bhattacharya
RB	Robert Bly
DC	Dilip Chitre
AC	Ananda Coomaraswamy
VD	Vidya Dehejia
HH & VNR	Hank Heifetz and Velcheru Narayana Rao
LH & SS	Linda Hess and Shukdeo Singh
JH	Jane Hirshfield
AK	Arun Kolatkar
DL & ECD	Denise Levertov and Edward C. Dimock Jr.
AKM	Arvind Krishna Mehrotra
WSM & JMM	W.S. Merwin and J. Moussaieff Masson
LN & CS	Leonard Nathan and Clinton Seely
GP	Gieve Patel
EP	Ezra Pound
AKR	A.K. Ramanujan
AS	Andrew Schelling
GS	Gary Snyder
CT & TKS	Chase Twichell and Tony K. Stewart

You, my messenger
are a tender sprig
but I trust you with a secret dispatch.
Go to the wind-tossed forest
where that dark man
awaits me.
Black clouds trouble the heavens,
spring breezes stir and the heart
also stirs.
But go to him safely.
May the gods keep a close
watch
over your art.

Śīlābhaṭṭārikā

:AS

LOVE

—— AND THE ——

TURNING
SEASONS

: Īśa Upaniṣad
(CIRCA 600 BCE)

1.

   The Great One dwells
in all this, and in all
that moves in this mobile universe.
Enjoy things by
giving them up, not by craving
some other man's
substance.

2.

   Engaged in works
hope to live
here for a hundred years—
it's what you receive,
nothing else.
There is no one for karma
to cling to.

3.

   There are worlds
they call sunless,
turbulent,
covered with gloom—
those who
violate spirit
depart after death
into them.

4.
    The Immobile One's
swifter than thought,
not even a god
can approach it.
Stands, yet outflanks what runs;
holds the waters
the Hidden Female let forth.

5.
    Moves,
and does not move.
Is distant,
is near.
Inhabits all this,
stays outside of it all.

6.
    Who sees
all breathing creatures
as spirit, spirit
in everything breathing,
no longer shrinks
from encounter.

7.
    When the spectator
of this unity
regards all creatures as Spirit,
who can suffer,
who be misled?

8.

    It is out traveling—
bright, bodiless, pure,
unflawed,
unpierced by evil. All objects
have in their self-nature
been arranged precisely about us
by that presence—
poet, and thinker.

9.

    They enter a turbulent
darkness, who
cultivate ignorance—
a yet thicker darkness
who are addicted to
knowledge.

10.

    It is different
from knowledge—different also
from what you do not know—
this we heard
from the steadfast ones
who opened our eyes.

11.

    Who is cunning
towards knowledge and ignorance,
with ignorance
moves across death,
with knowledge reaches
the deathless.

12.
   They enter a turbulent
darkness, who
cultivate unmanifest worlds—
a yet thicker darkness
who are addicted
to empirical worlds.

13.
   Different
from what you can see—
different also
from what goes unseen—
this we heard
from the steadfast ones
who opened our eyes.

14.
   Who is cunning
towards loss and creation,
with loss
crosses death,
with creation reaches
the deathless.

15.
   A golden solar disc
hides the gateway
into the Real—
remove it O Nourisher,
so I can see
the Unwavering.

16.

    O Nourisher, sole Seer,
judge of the dead,
O sun, offspring of the Father of Creatures,
fan out your rays,
draw up luster.
    That most
splendrous form, yours—
I would see—that is—
the *I am*.

17.

Animate breath
    is undying
but the body ends in cinder.
Om!
    Oh volition, remember,
remember that which was done.
Remember
that which was
done.

18.

    O Fire,
knower of every creature's breath,
take us along the good road,
far from deviant evil.
We offer you
    precious verse.

                                             :AS

Īśa Upaniṣad

INDIA'S ONE HUNDRED and eight Upaniṣads are an enormous compendium of cosmic speculation, folklore, mystical insight, and homespun humor. They range in length from Īśa's eighteen brief stanzas to book-size treatises. Some interpret complex yoga formulas, others lay forth solar and lunar paths to follow after death. They are laced with stinging anticlerical diatribes, and contain vast open spaces for the mind. Scholars, gurus, and poets—including William Butler Yeats, who worked with a Vedantist friend—have chosen and translated ones they consider the principal, the oldest, or the most significant, generally ten or fifteen.

The term *upaniṣad* means "sit down near." It refers to a period of spiritual upheaval in the first millennium BCE when the early Vedic religion came to seem outmoded. Priests dominated the spiritual landscape, requiring payment to perform the necessary sacraments of birth-names, initiation, marriage, and funeral rites. Complicated rituals enveloped the calendar, along with horse sacrifices, prayer beads, fire ceremonies, payment to priests in cattle, and a pantheon of nature deities that left the significant philosophical questions unanswered. Alienated seekers left the towns and cities in large numbers to collect around teachers in the forest. They lived simply, or founded retreat centers—where they swapped ideas, held debates, posed questions, and struggled toward a renewed sense of spirit.

The verses of Īśa, "The Great One," lie among the oldest strata of the Upaniṣads. Scholars generally place it six to eight centuries BCE, though I suspect most of its stanzas are rooted deeper, maybe circulating orally for centuries before someone brought them together. They read like snatches of song from some very distant yogins, passed on as fragments of a large tradition, and eventually—like the lyrics of many folksong and spiritual traditions—brought to rest in a context or "text" where they seem to fit. The stanzas were almost certainly cobbled together from several sources: a bricolage more than a treatise. In the original Sanskrit, shifting rhythms, an archaic vocabulary, statements that resemble riddles, and quick dialectical turns of phrase give the piece a strikingly postmodern ring. So does the use of a neuter pronoun "that"—not masculine or feminine—for the great one, addressed as "poet, and thinker."

Īśa's fragmentary utterances on knowledge and ignorance, the visible and the invisible, seem to echo from another life. Toward the final verse rises a cry for vision: it starts as a plea to remove the "golden solar disc" that holds back the truth. Its crescendo seems to reach for some far limit of human speech. With no named author or visible poet attached, the whole thing possibly came together as a funerary chant. The closing stanzas are for the burning grounds: *Animate breath / is undying / but the body ends in cinder*. One can read Īśa Upaniṣad as a breath of the archaic—in contrast to the personal tone, so individuated, so fierce with emotion, of India's bhakti poetry, the vernacular song that would sweep India two thousand years later.

: Sanskrit Poems

(circa sixth—twelfth centuries)

Krishna went out to play
Mother
and he ate dirt

Is that true Krishna

No
who said it

Your brother Balarāma

Not true
Look at my face

Open your mouth

    he opened it
    and she stood speechless

    inside was
    the universe

    may he protect you

Caṇḍaka

:WSM & JMM

Between his hands
Krishna takes
Yaśodhā's breast
in his mouth takes
her nipple
at once he remembers
in an earlier life taking
to his mouth the conch shell
to call to battle
all bow down now to
the thought of his skin
at that moment.

from the *Kāvyaprakāśa*

:WSM & JMM

The goddess Laksmi
loves to make love to Vishnu
from on top
looking down she sees in his navel
a lotus
and on it Brahmā the god
but she can't bear to stop
so she puts her hand
over Vishnu's right eye
which is the sun
and night comes on
and the lotus closes
with Brahmā inside

from the *Kāvyaprakāśa*

:WSM & JMM

Friend
I am cursed

may or may not see him again

yet by itself
sound of his flute if into my ears should fall

enough

Anonymous

:WSM & JMM

Holy sixth day
in the woods they worship the
trees then
then my heart beat hard
at how far I was going into
the woods
a snake appeared in front of me
and I fell down
I started writhing and rolling
this way and that way
my dress fell off
my hair burned along
my back
thorns scratched me
everywhere
suddenly who am I
who was I
how I
love those celebrations

Govindasvāmin

:WSM & JMM

Oh friend you
play in the mud like a child
your blouse not
even covering your breasts
your father the cowherd
thinking you still a child
has done nothing
to find you a husband
but then suddenly
your eyelids leap as you hear
in the Vṛnda forest the sound
of Krishna's flute
and you tremble with longing
and show the whites of your eyes

Anonymous

:WSM & JMM

Anyone would think
I alone
had been unfaithful
what did you
feel inside you
when you heard the flute
Krishna was playing
and no woman said no

Anonymous

:WSM & JMM

Sanskrit Poems

O N THE SURFACE, Sanskrit classical poetry looks resolutely secular, the bulk of it being love poetry. The poets worked with *rasa*, bedrock emotions, which they considered parallel to spiritual states of being. They also lived in a landscape full of deities, mythologies, and mysteries; they could not keep the gods out.

I cannot locate any information on Caṇḍaka except that he may have been Kashmiri. His theme is an old story, familiar through India, an episode from Krishna's childhood. In J. Moussaieff Masson's words, "the emphasis is on the elusiveness of the epiphany," the poem depicting "Kṛṣṇa as a young boy, impetuous, playful, disdainful of his elders, who at a given moment allows them an insight into his mystery."

Nothing is known of the other poets. The verse on the baby Krishna taking his foster mother's breast refers to his role in a former lifetime (the gods too reincarnate) as charioteer in the great battle known from the Bhagavad-gītā. In those days all warriors of note carried a conch shell into the fight. The verse appears in a poetics textbook. So does the one on Laksmi and Vishnu's lovemaking. Masson after commenting on a few of the more evident aspects of the latter poem writes, "I suspect that there is something further in this verse that I . . . am missing." Maybe its author wove a cryptic symbolism through the images, meant to cast the reader into a yogic or mystical state of mind.

In the remaining poems the flute is Krishna's. At the soft forest notes of his bamboo flute the women of Vrindavana itch to leave their houses and join him in the woods, for a night of dancing and lovemaking. I have read anthropologists who believe Krishna's flute is a holdover from pastoral nomads, or even Ice Age migrations. Its intoxicating notes (sometimes given as seven) draw the settled, agrarian women from their homes. The flute not only arouses erotic and spiritual desire, it raises longings for the lifestyle of an earlier era, free from village life, with its settled families, tedious daily rounds, hard labor, and continual anxiety about the weather.

: Manikkavacakar
(ninth century)

He grabbed me
    lest I go astray.

Wax before an unspent fire,
    mind melted,
    body trembled.

I bowed, I wept,
    danced, and cried aloud,
    I sang, and I praised him.

Unyielding, as they say,
    as an elephant's jaw
    or a woman's grasp,
    was love's unrelenting
    seizure.

Love pierced me
    like a nail
    driven into a green tree.

Overflowing, I tossed
    like a sea,

heart growing tender,
body shivering,

while the world called me Demon!
and laughed at me,

I left shame behind,

took as an ornament
    the mockery of local folk.
Unswerving, I lost my cleverness
    in the bewilderment of ecstasy.

:AKR

Manikkavacakar

IN MANIKKAVACAKAR'S POEM, composed in Tamil, note not only the dance, but the way the poet performs his dance at the center of his own poem. "I bowed, I wept, / danced, cried aloud, / I sang, and I praised him." Manikkavacakar speaks from the center of the poem, but more than that, the poem declares his personal experience of the god's power. Here is the link back to a most archaic visionary condition, well-documented in pan-Asiatic shamanism and folklore—a state of intoxication with the divine. The poem points forward also, to what lies at the heart of India's bhakti traditions: an individual, unique relationship with the god. Feel the visceral force of what happens: "Love pierced me / like a nail / driven into a green tree." Then a declaration that recurs throughout bhakti: "I left shame behind." Lal Ded, Mirabai, Tukaram, and the Bauls all echo the statement in their own fashion.

: ĀṆṬĀḶ

(FIRST HALF OF THE NINTH CENTURY)

We rose before dawn
to praise you,
bringing our song to your Lotus Feet—
hear what we ask!
Please listen,
you who were born among us
into this cowherding clan—
What choice do you have
but to take us into your service,
your heartfelt servants, your kin?
We didn't come to receive the outer drum,
the drum of a day, O Govinda—
We are yours for life.
Make all our desires be for you,
it is you alone that we want. Hear our song!

:JH

O ancient one,
I wrote your name
upon the wall.
For you I drew the sugarcane bow,
banner with emblem of fish,
attendant maidens,
retinue of horses.
From early childhood
I yearned for
the lord of Dvārka,
adored him alone,
dedicated to him
my budding breasts.
Kāmadeva, unite me to him soon.

:VD

I dedicated my swelling breasts
to the lord who holds
the conch and flaming discus.
If there is even a whisper
of giving me to a mortal,
I shall not live.
O Manmatha,
would you permit a roving jackal
to sniff and eat
the sacrificial food
the Brahmins offer
to celestial gods?

:VD

Learned Brahmins
chanted Vedic mantras,
placed green *dharba* grass
around the sacrificial fire
lit with twigs.
The lord of great prowess,
strong as a raging elephant,
took my hand,
we walked around the fire—
I dreamt this dream, my friend.

:VD

My soul melts in anguish—
he cares not
if I live or die.
If I see the lord of Govardhana
that looting thief,
that plunderer,
I shall pluck
by their roots
these useless breasts,
I shall fling them
at his chest,
I shall cool
the raging fire
within me.

:VD

To soothe the grief
of my rounded breasts,
is it not better
in this very birth
to serve Govinda
in little intimate ways,
than wait for a life beyond?
If one day
he would fold me
into his radiant chest,
that would fulfill me.
Else, looking straight at me,
uttering the truth,
he should give me
leave to go—
that also I would accept.

:VD

Āṇṭāḷ

"IN THE TAMIL country of South India, between the sixth and tenth centuries, there emerged a remarkable group of holy men and women who transformed the milieu of the south. Blazing a trail for the path of love, they emphasized surrender to a personal god. . . . " The translator and art critic Vidya Dehejia opens her book of Āṇṭāḷ's poetry with these fairy-tale-like words, highlighting the Alvar poets' extraordinary immersion in spiritual love. *Alvar* means "immersed." Of these poets, twelve in number, Āṇṭāḷ is the lone woman.

Āṇṭāḷ—a name or title that means "she who is victorious"—is the most celebrated woman poet of the Tamil language. The likeliest date for her is the opening half of the ninth century. Scholars have placed her as early as the seventh and as late as the thirteenth, though—calculating various dates from a few brief lines in her poetry that refer to an astrological event:

> Venus has risen
> Jupiter has gone to his sleep

The account of Āṇṭāḷ's life of reckless devotion come from two hagiographies, one classical Tamil, the other Sanskrit. They recount how the priest Vishnucitta—himself a devotional poet—was one day hoeing the ground for his *tulsi* or holy basil, a plant used throughout India medicinally and as a tonic, but also identified with Krishna and central to the ceremonials of certain holy days. With a turn of his hoe Vishnucitta uncovered a baby girl embedded in the soil of his garden. Bringing her home, he named her Kotai, "Fragrant Braids"—her hair emitted the fragrance of basil—and raised her as though she were "an incarnation of Bhudevi," the earth goddess.

During her childhood Kotai took to dressing up as a bride when her father was absent, winding in her hair the flower garland prepared for evening worship of Krishna. She would study herself at length before a glass, imagining herself Krishna's bride. Then, violating standards of purity, after using the garland for her own ornamentation she would return it to its place for use in the evening's service. One day her father happened on her dress-up game; he was horrified at the desecration and withheld the garland from that evening's worship. During the night Vishnu appeared in a dream to him, declaring that the garland Kotai had worn was made fragrant and holy by her hair.

Āṇṭāḷ became obsessed with Krishna, meditating on him and composing two collections of poetry. Her father—perplexed at what was in store when Āṇṭāḷ rejected any suggestion of a human husband—had another dream visitation by Vishnu. This time the god informed Vishnucitta that he intended to marry Āṇṭāḷ. The clan prepared a sumptuous marriage ceremony and carried Āṇṭāḷ to a Vishnu temple at Rankanata. There Vishnu was depicted reclining on a great serpent that drifted on the ocean of existence. Āṇṭāḷ climbed from the palanquin, approached the god's image, and embraced his feet. Then she climbed onto the serpent-couch with him and vanished.

This absorption of Āṇṭāḷ's physical body into the god is the first instance I know of in the chronicles of bhakti. Later bhakti poets similarly disappear: Mirabai, Muktabai, and Lal Ded among them.

The first poem given here is from the *Tiruppavai,* a sequence of thirty poems. Tamil girls have sung these since Āṇṭāḷ's time, in worship of Vishnu during the month of Markali, the lunar month that ranges from mid-December to mid-January. The songs point to Krishna's birth into a cowherd clan, and call him by many names including the affectionate "Govinda," which identifies the blue god as a protector of cattle. The other poems come from the fourteen-canto *Nacciyar Tirumoli*, "The Anguish of Separation." Separation from one's lover had been a recurrent theme in India's love poetry, but Āṇṭāḷ's immediacy and feverish desperation inflame her verses; she rips the terms of love out of the realm of aesthetics, and casts the singer and listeners directly into Krishna's presence. Bridesmaids in Tamil Nadu still sing the *Tiruppavai* at weddings.

: NAMMALVAR
(CIRCA 880—930)

What She Said

Evening has come,
   but not the Dark One.

The bulls,
   their bells jingling,
   have mated with the cows
and the cows are frisky.

The flutes play cruel songs,
   bees flutter in their bright
   white jasmine
   and the blue-black lily.

The sea leaps into the sky
   and cries aloud.

Without him here,
   what shall I say?
   how shall I survive?

:AKR

What Her Mother Said

O women,
    you too have daughters
    and have brought them up.

    How can I tell you
    about my poor girl?

    She talks of the conch shell,
    she talks of the wheel,
    and she talks, night and day,
    of the basil in his hair,

what shall I do?

:AKR

You roam the seas
    the mountains, the skies,
you touch them lightly,

cold north wind!

Night and day,
    lit by alternate lamps
       of sun and moon,
like us
you wander sleepless:

are you also craving,
since the time
    time began,

for a glimpse
    of our lord of the mighty wheel?

: AKR

What She Said to Her Girlfriend

Dear friend,
    dear as the Dark One's paradise,

night grows long, many lives long,
    when we part;
or goes fast, a split second many times split,
    when we are together.

So I suffer even when my lover joins me
    many nights in a row,
and suffer again
    when he goes away.

Blessed night, ever flowing,
    is full of tricks,
      plays fast and loose.

:AKR

My lord
    who swept me away forever
        into joy that day,

made me over into himself

and sang in Tamil
his own songs
through me:

what shall I say
    to the first of things,
        flame
        standing there,

what shall I say
    to stop?

:AKR

Nammalvar

O F T H E T W E L V E Krishna poets known as Alvars, who com-
posed in Tamil between the sixth and ninth centuries, Nammal-
var is considered the greatest. Called by a variety of names including
Maran and Catakopan, to most people he holds the affectionate title
Nammalvar, "our own Alvar." Historians propose 880 and 930 CE as
his dates. Nammalvar's songs—supposedly sung forth in one grand
recitation without forethought or revision—come grouped into tens,
the tens into hundreds, and finally into a thousand. These numbers
are more symbolic than actual, as each gathering includes a *phalaśruti*
verse, or "recital of the fruits," an account of the merit derived by
singing the stanzas. The actual count of verses is 1,102.

Born in the village of Tirukurukur, Tamil Nadu, of peasant caste,
Nammalvar was unresponsive or catatonic at birth. His mother
offered her breast but the infant did not respond. He lay as though
mute and deaf, neither whimpered nor smiled, would not move his
limbs, but lay wherever his parents placed him, motionless. Con-
founded and distraught, in an act of despair they took the child to
a nearby statue of Vishnu and left him at the god's pedestal. The boy
rose to his feet—the first act of his own volition—strode to an old
nearby tamarind tree, climbed into a hollow in the trunk, and, closing
his eyes, took the seated posture of a yogin.

Meanwhile, far to the north, a wandering poet named Maturakavi
was pilgrimaging on the bank of the Ganges. In the southern sky a
bright star flared; Maturakavi took the astronomical event as pro-
phetic. For three nights and days the poet followed the star, which led
him to Tirukurukur where he found the child, motionless as a basalt
statue, seated inside the tamarind. Maturakavi tried to rouse the boy,

shouting, gesturing, knocking stones against a nearby temple wall. The boy never moved.

Finally the pilgrim approached the hollow in the tree and cried loudly, "Master! If the spirit is sheathed in matter, what does it eat, where does it rest?"

"*That* it will eat, and *there* it rests," came the child's instant reply.

The spirit feeds on *that*, the holy. It rests *there*, in the sphere of the sacred.

With this declaration the boy's voice broke open and he sang forth the verses of the *Tiruvaymoli*, or "Holy Word of Mouth." These spontaneous verses, not the product of forethought or labor, became known as "the ocean of the Tamil Veda, in which the Upaniṣads of the thousand rivers drain." It is a single unbroken poem, each hymn or stanza linked to the previous by opening with that verse's final word.

The child poet had studied no grammars, trained himself in no poetic theory, learnt no scripture, sat at the feet of no guru. His songs erupted at the moment of ripeness, interlinked, complete, and without revision.

Though the *Tiruvaymoli* is a single poem, individual verses stand by themselves, and regularly get recited as separate hymns. Dramatic voices emerge, in particular the singer taking the voice of an adolescent girl, longing for her lover or destroyed by his negligence. The lover is Krishna, and his *līlā* or divine play lies at the root of both heartbreak and rapture, two primary modes of spiritual perception.

: Mahādēviyakka
(twelfth century)

So long as this breath fills your nostrils,
Why seek out fragrant flowers?

Peaceful, compassionate, patient, already your own master,
Why do you need to cross your legs to Know?

Once the entire world is yourself,
What could a life of solitude add?

O white Jasmine Lord—

:JH

When I am hungry,
The villagers
Fill my begging bowl
With rice.

Thirsty, I turn toward
The cattle troughs, wells,
And streams.

For my sleep,
Abandoned temples
Are blanket enough.

And when I am lonely,
O white Jasmine Lord,
My soul deepens
with You.

:JH

When the body becomes Your mirror,
how can it serve?

When the mind becomes Your mind,
what is left to remember?

Once my life is Your gesture,
how can I pray?

When all my awareness is Yours,
what can there be to know?

I became You, Lord, and forgot You.

:JH

(On Her Decision to Stop Wearing Clothes)

Coins in the hand
Can be stolen,
But who can rob this body
Of its own treasure?

The last thread of clothing
Can be stripped away,
But who can peel off Emptiness,
That nakedness covering all?

Fools, while I dress
In the Jasmine Lord's morning light,
I cannot be shamed—
What would you have me hide under silk
And the glitter of jewels?

:JH

A vein of sapphires
hides in the earth,
a sweetness in fruit;

and in plain-looking rock
lies a golden ore,
and in seeds,
the treasure of oil.

Like these,
the Infinite
rests concealed in the heart.

No one can see the ways
of our jasmine-white Lord.

:JH

Not one, not two, not three or four,
but through eighty-four thousand vaginas
have I come,
            I have come
through unlikely worlds,
                        guzzled on
pleasure and pain.
                    Whatever be
all previous lives,
                    show me mercy
this one day,
            O lord
            white as jasmine.

Would a circling surface vulture
   know such depths of sky
   as the moon would know?

would a weed on the riverbank
   know such depths of water
   as the lotus would know?

would a fly darting nearby
   know the smell of flowers
   as the bee would know?

O lord white as jasmine
   only you would know
   the way of your devotees:
   how would these,

these
   mosquitoes
   on the buffalo's hide?

:AKR

Husband inside,
lover outside.
I can't manage them both.

This world
and that other,
cannot manage them both.

O lord white as jasmine

I cannot hold in one hand
both the round nut
and the long bow.

:AKR

Who cares
    who strips a tree of leaf
    once the fruit is plucked?

Who cares
    who lies with a woman
    you have left?

Who cares
    who ploughs the land
    you have abandoned?

After this body has known my lord
    who cares if it feeds
    a dog
    or soaks up water?

:AKR

People,
male and female,
blush when a cloth covering their shame
comes loose.
    When the lord of lives
lives drowned without a face
in the world, how can you be modest?

When all the world is the eye of the lord,
onlooking everywhere, what can you
cover and conceal?

:AKR

Make me go from house to house
    with arms stretched for alms.

If I beg, make them give nothing.

If they give, make it fall to the ground.

If it falls, before I pick it up, make a dog take it,

O lord
white as jasmine.

:AKR

Riding the blue sapphire mountains
wearing moonstone for slippers
blowing long horns
O Śiva
when shall I
crush you on my pitcher breasts

O lord white as jasmine
when do I join you
stripped of body's shame
and heart's modesty?

:AKR

If He says
He has to go away
to fight battles at the front
   I understand and can be quiet.

But how can I bear it
when He is here in my hands
right here in my heart
   and will not take me?

O mind, O memory of pasts,
if you will not help me get to Him
how can I ever bear it?

:AKR

Mahādēviyakka

MAHĀDĒVIYAKKA BELONGED to an outspoken, antiortho-
dox group of poets who sang or wrote in Kannada, a language
of Dravidian stock, spoken in the southern state of Mysore. Col-
lectively these poets are called Vīraśaiva—heroic Śiva worshippers.
Each poet's *vacana*s or "poems" carry an identifying signature line,
an *aṅkita*, which bears not the poet's name but the name of one of
Śiva's specific local forms. You can identify the poet by the form of
Śiva he or she sings to. Mahādēviyakka, born in the twelfth century,
was initiated at the age of ten by an unknown guru, and from then
on considered her lover to be Mallikārjuna, a form of Śiva housed in
her home village of Uḍutaḍi. A.K. Ramanujan translates the name—
Mallika (jasmine), Arjuna (white)—"lord white as jasmine."

Renowned for her beauty and sparkling intelligence, but pledg-
ing herself to her god, Mahādēvi (*akka*, elder sister, is an honorary
title) refused the advances of human suitors. A local chieftain named
Kausika finally took her for his wife, but the marriage was doomed.
Some of her poems play on the friction between her divine lover and
her mortal husband.

> Mother,
> because they all have thorns
> in their chests,
>   I cannot take
> any man in my arms but my lord
> white as jasmine.
> (AKR translation)

Shortly after her wedding, Mahādēvi deserted her husband, her family, and her social ties, and took to wandering, intoxicated by god. Defiant in the face of social convention, particularly any oppressive to women, she shed her clothes, covering herself with long tresses of raven-black hair. She made her way to the city of Kalyana, where two older Vīraśaiva poets had formed a spiritual community founded on equality and fierce resistance to orthodox religion.

One of these poets, Allama, received Mahādēvi in quarters they called the Hall of Experience. The ensuing conversation—seasoned skeptical guru examining wildly passionate young visitor—became notable in Vīraśaiva lore. Mahādēviyakka's surviving songs seem to stem from these dialogues. Allama asked to whom she was married; her reply: "the White Jasmine Lord." One inevitable question was why she would throw off her clothes, as though she could shed illusion along with her raiment. Then, if free from human convention, why veil herself in hair? Her reply:

> Till the fruit is ripe inside
> the skin will not fall off.
> I'd a feeling it would hurt you
> if I displayed the body's seals of love.
> O brother, don't tease me
> needlessly. I'm given entire
> into the hands of my lord
> white as jasmine.
> (AKR translation)

A.K. Ramanujan calls Mahādēviyakka a "love-child." In the early 1970s at the University of Chicago, where he produced his translations, he must have thought the students on campus looked just like her. In her own time, the Vīraśaivas regarded Mahādēviyakka as the most accomplished of poets and the one with deepest insight. Her *vacana*s are not rustic or unstudied. They depict the phases of love found in Sanskrit poetry and drama, and speak of adulterous love with a secret partner, of insufferable hours when her lover is absent, and of rapture at sexual union. "In her," Ramanujan writes, "the phases of human love are metaphors for the phases of mystic ascent."

: LAL DED
(EARLY FOURTEENTH CENTURY)

Beneath you yawns a pit.
How can you dance over it,
how can you gather belongings?
There's nothing you can take with you.
How can you even
savor food or drink?

: AS

I have seen an educated man starve,
a leaf blown off by bitter wind.
Once I saw a thoughtless fool
beat his cook.
Lalla has been waiting
for the allure of the world
to fall away.

:AS

This world,
compared to You—

a lake so tiny
even a mustard seed
is too large for it to hold.

Yet from that lake all Beings drink.

And into it deer, jackals,
rhinoceri, sea-elephants falling.

From the earliest moment of birth,
falling and falling
in You.

:JH

I searched for my Self
until I grew weary,

but no one, I know now,
reaches the hidden knowledge
by means of effort.

Then, absorbed in "Thou art This,"
I found the place of Wine.

There all the jars are filled,
but no one is left to drink.

:JH

Ocean and the mind are alike.
Under the ocean
flames *vadvagni*, the world-destroying fire.
In man's heart twists the
flame of rage.
When that one bursts forth,
its searing words of wrath and abuse
scorch everything.
If you weigh the words
calmly, though, imperturbably,
you'll see they have no substance,
no weight.

:AS

It provides your body clothes.
It wards off the cold.
It needs only scrub and water to survive.
Who instructed you, O Brahmin,
to cut this sheep's throat—
to placate a lifeless stone?

:AS

I might scatter the southern clouds,
drain the sea, or cure someone
hopelessly ill.
But to change the mind
of a fool
is beyond me.

:AS

I came by the public road
but won't return on it.
On the embankment I stand, halfway
through the journey.
Day is gone. Night has fallen.
I dig in my pockets but can't find a
cowry shell.
What can I pay for the ferry?

:AS

The god is stone.
The temple is stone.
Top to bottom everything's stone.
What are you praying to,
learned man?
Can you harmonize
your five bodily breaths
with the mind?

:AS

You are the earth, the sky,
the air, the day, the night.
You are the grain
the sandalwood paste
the water, flowers, and all else.
What could I possibly bring
as an offering?

:AS

Solitary, I roamed the width of Space,
and left trickery behind.
The place of the hidden Self
unfolded and out
of the muck,
a milk-white lotus.

:AS

To learn the scriptures is easy,
to live them, hard.
The search for the Real
is no simple matter.

Deep in my looking,
the last words vanished.
Joyous and silent,
the waking that met me there.

:JH

O Blue-Throated God
I have the same six constituents as you,
yet separate from you
I'm miserable.
Here's the difference—
you have mastered the six
I've been robbed by them.

The six *kancuka*s, "husks" or "coverings" of existence in Kashmir Śaivism:
appearance, form, time, knowledge, passion, fate.

:AS

I, Lalla, entered
the gate of the mind's garden and saw
Śiva united with Śaktī.
I was immersed in the lake of undying bliss.
Here, in this lifetime,
I've been unchained from the wheel
of birth and death.
What can the world do to me?

‡AS

Lal Ded

L AL DED was born in Kashmir early in the 1300s, probably to parents of some Hindu persuasion. Her *vākh* (verses, sayings) suggest an early education in her father's house and eventual marriage into a Brahman family of Pampor, where her mother-in-law treated her with dispiriting cruelty. Lalla, as she calls herself in the signature line of her poems, took to visiting the nearby river each morning—traditional for an Indian woman who went to fetch the household's water. But Lalla would cross the river secretly, maybe by ferry, to worship Naṭa Keśava Bhairava, a form of Śiva, in his temple situated on the far bank. Her mother-in-law, noticing her long absences, suspected her of infidelity. Rivers in Indian lore, particularly their shaded riparian groves and stands of tall, concealing rushes, are in convention the site of clandestine trysts. Lal Ded's husband became soured by his mother's suspicion and one day when Lalla entered the house with a pot of water on her head, struck it with his staff in a fit of violent jealousy. The earthenware jug shattered but the water remained "frozen" in place, atop her head, until Lalla had poured it into the household containers. A little leftover water she tossed out the door where it formed a miraculous lake, said to exist in the early twentieth century, but dry today.

Lalla's reputation spread, based on a series of miracles she performed. People began to seek her out for assistance or simply to take *darshan*, that specifically Indian practice in which blessings come to a person who ceremonially takes sight of a deity, a saint, or a spiritual teacher. Lal Ded's love of solitude was compromised by all the attention and the rancor in her house. She left her graceless marriage and took up the homeless life. Legend, based on the following verse, has it that she went forth naked, dancing on the roads, singing her *vākh*.

> My guru gave a single precept:
> turn your gaze from outside to inside
> fix it on the hidden self.
> I, Lalla, took this to heart
> and naked set forth to dance—
> (AS translation)

One Muslim chronicler says she danced in ecstasy "like the Hebrew *nabis* of old and the more recent Dervishes." Islamic writers chronicle her encounters with their holy men, while Hindu texts tell of gurus. The Kashmir of her day held Buddhists, Nath yogins, Brahman teachers, Sufis, and Tantric adepts. She may have learnt something from each of them. Still, she seems to have considered herself a dedicated Śaivite yogini (practitioner dedicated to Śiva); tales of insight and supernatural power surpassing that of her instructors began to circulate. Yet records of her don't appear until centuries after her death, nor has anyone found manuscripts containing her *vākh* that date from anywhere near her lifetime.

Circulating oral stories make a good deal of her decision to live without clothing; this made her a spectacle at times. She was taunted. Jane Hirshfield tells the story of children pestering her, and a silk merchant who came to her defense with bundles of cloth. Taking two bolts of silk of equal weight, Lal Ded placed one on each shoulder and went on her way. "As she went through the day, each time someone ridiculed her, she tied a knot in the cloth on her left shoulder; each time someone praised her, she tied a knot in the cloth on the right. At day's end, she returned to the merchant, and asked him to weigh the bundles again. She thanked him for his earlier concern, but also pointed out that, as he could see for himself, nothing had changed."

Whether blame or praise came her way, the bundles remained equal in weight.

Around the age of fifty Lal Ded sang some verses and a crowd gathered. On finishing she climbed into a large earthen pot and pulled another huge pot over her head. When she did not reemerge the spectators separated the two containers. She had vanished—as had Āṇṭāḷ before her, and as Mirabai and Muktabai would in years to come.

: Dhūrjaṭi

(SIXTEENTH CENTURY)

My chest has been worn away
by the breasts of women rubbing against it.
My skin has been roughened
with love scars from their nails.
Lost in the straining of passion, youth
has gone.
My hair has started falling out,
I'm sick of it all.
I can't go on in this circling world,
God of Kāḷahasti, make me
      desireless.

:HH & VNR

Saying this is your wife, they bring a woman
and the knots are tied at the neck.
Then children come one after another
and the boys take their brides
and the girls are given in marriage.
O God of Kāḷahasti,
how did you fashion this worthless wheel
of family love that turns us,
cog meshing smoothly with cog around
and around?

:HH & VNR

When mourners cry out over the dead
burning on the river bank, they will say,
"O God of Death! We are coming,
we as well, you can be sure of us,
we know it!" Then they take the cleansing bath
and the fools move on and they forget
the real weight of what they have said.
O God of Kāḷahasti

:HH & VNR

How can you be praised in elaborate language,
similes, conceits, overtones, secondary meanings,
or textures of sound? They cannot contain
your form. Enough of them!
More than enough. Can poetry hold out
before the face of truth?
Ah, but we poets,
O God of Kāḷahasti,
why don't we feel any shame?

:HH & VNR

In town after town,
men who sing ordinary songs
now call themselves poets.
They go into places and explain their
     songs to somebody
they happen to find
and they say to them,
"You are aesthetes! You know poetry!"
O God of Kāḷahasti,
substance and emptiness are not distinguished.
Poetry has been cheapened.
Where is it
good poets can go?

:HH & VNR

When I think of the past,
the terrible sinful
things I have done,
I am sickened by them.
When I see before me
that grim death after death
will come to me sooner or later,
I am frightened.
When I look at myself,
when I think of my actions,
terror descends upon me and
darkness falls across time.
O God of Kāḷahasti

:HH & VNR

I have had my satisfaction
with pleasures at the doorway of the King of Love
and those that have come to me through entering
the palace gates of many kings.
Now I want quiet. Show me
the doorway to the highest truth
where, through your kindness,
O God of Kāḷahasti,
I can be at ease and at rest.

HH & VNR

Dhūrjaṭi

IN THE STATE of Andhra Pradesh, on the bank of a river known as the Mogileru, sits the small town of Kāḷahasti. A temple with fortified walls, placed on a hill that commands a view of the surrounding country, is dedicated to Śrī Kāḷahasti Īśvara, the town's resident god. The name is an odd amalgam of words for spider, snake, and elephant, three creatures that figure prominently in local stories about Lord Śiva. Kāḷahasti is the regional manifestation of Śiva.

Somewhere in the mid-sixteenth century the poet Dhūrjaṭi arrived at the temple. Of Dhūrjaṭi's biography hardly anything survives except what one can glean from his poetry. He composed a long ornate poem in Telugu court style (Telugu is the language of Andhra and several surrounding states). In them Dhūrjaṭi celebrates the Kāḷahasti temple, recounting in detail the legends attached to it. The poem's colophon carries his name; the poem's flourishes, laden with Sanskrit-style compound words, shows Dhūrjaṭi had trained as a court poet. Tradition assigns to him one further work, the *Kāḷahastīśvara Śatakamu*, or Hundred Poems to Lord Kāḷahasti. In this collection his anger and contempt, leveled at misguided pride and the terrible pettiness of rulers, sound so genuine they must reflect his personal experience. The translators consider this "hundred poems" an "emotional autobiography." It lacks fact, episode, human names, but comes laced with passionate devotion and a fierce despair at worldly attachment. He levels particular anger at sexual vanity and the abuse of political power.

The *śatakam*, a collection of a hundred poems (the Victorian British called them "centuries"), shows up all over India. Dozens if not hundreds occur in Sanskrit, Tamil, Telugu, and the literary vernaculars. The number one hundred is more symbolic than actual; most collections contain a few more, a few less. (One hundred and eight, a magical number for Hindus, Buddhists, and others, is common.) Dhūrjaṭi's collection may hold 116 poems; no scholar has sifted through and compiled a critical edition. Telugu speakers chant its verses, so Dhūrjaṭi's work remains active, quick to rise to those dissatisfied with worldly goals or the political power structure.

The name Dhūrjaṭi, Twisted Locks, would be the name for a Śiva devotee. Śiva, as well as his sadhus—scary mendicants who sometimes follow extreme yoga practices—wear dreadlocks twisted into ropes, matted with cow dung. Some cake their locks with ash from the burning ground. These sadhus reject family and caste identity, saying they belong to the lineage of Śiva. Which may be why Dhūrjaṭi in the end left nothing but his poems.

> I never think of asking you to give me things,
> so if you don't care for my poetry
> I'll bear that all right.
> It's only my tongue's natural work,
> nothing other than my worship.
> (HH & VNR translation)

⠇ JÑANDEV

(1275—1296)

Blue is this sky, a blue filled with love,
Blue is this entire symmetry.

A blue being-in-itself, the blue of all karma,
I see a blue Guru in his blue resort.

Bluely I behave, I eat blue,
I see blueness in a blue sort of way.

Jñandev has entered the loving embrace
Of the blue cowherd in the school of blue.

⠂DC

The quintessence of awareness,
The knowledge of infinity,
The one whom the sky clothes,
Who has no form, no colour, nor property:

That graceful One, Hari, the reliever:
I've seen Him filling my eyes!
Seeing Him, I've set aside
Even the act of seeing!

Says Jñandev, inside any flame is
The Self's very own flame:
And that flame is imaged here
Standing on The Brick!

Shall I call you the formed One?
Shall I call you the formless?
The formed and the unformed is
Only the one Govind!

He cannot be deduced
He cannot be conceived
The Shrutis say,
"He's not such; nor even such."

Shall I call You the vastest One?
Shall I call You the minutest One?
The vast and the minute
Are only One Govind.

Shall I call You the visible One?
Shall I call You the invisible One?
Both the visible and the invisible
Are the only One Govind.

By the blessing of Nivrutti,
Jñandev speaks,
"Our great parent, husband of the Goddess Rakhuma, is
Vithal."

:DC

: Muktabai

(1279—1297)

the zoom ant
swallowed the sun
the barren woman
begot a son

a scorpion went
to the lower depths
shesha bowed to him
with a thousand heads

a pregnant fly
delivered a kite
having seen it all
mukta smiled

                                                            :AK

When one looks beyond the void,
There is not even a void left.
The one who sees keeps what's seen
In one's own place.

O mother mine! What a great saviour this!
The One who illuminates All!
He appeared in Pandharpur
Bringing Vaikunth down with Himself!

One does not know where He will go—
Being, becoming, and vanishing at will!
The resonance of the Shrutis is thus realized:
"*Not such is the One; nor such is the One.*"

Muktai is filled with love.
Vithal amazes her.
The mattress is emptiness.
Lie down upon emptiness.

:DC

From Muktabai's Dialogue with the Super-Yogi Changdev

"Tell me where the Self is in its dreaming state.
And how does it continue to chase us even then?"

Says Changa, "O lady, Muktabai, will you explain to me
How illusion finds a real home in the human body?"

"Your body creates chaos," Says Mukta to Changa,
"Try dwelling in your inner self with a strong will.

"It's neither bound nor free
It's neither real nor is it illusory

"It's not different from you, so what difference can it make to you?
Does the real dwell in the body or is it illusory?"

Changa asks, "Tell me O Muktai.
What dwells in the body? The real or the illusory?"

"There's no pleasure in the Self, nor is there pain; there's no virtue,
    nor sin;
No *karma*, no *dharma*; for nothing is ever conceived there.

"There's no bond; so there's nothing to be liberated;
O Vateshvar! There's no Supreme Reality," says Mukta, the born
    siddha,

"If you show me gold, I can test it.
Show me your own experience in what you say!

"The human mind is stubbornly egocentric. But where are *you*
If there's no *me?*" Muktai asks.

"The egoist's *mantra* is '*I am the Supreme Being.*'" Says Muktai to
    Changa,
"*Me* is my anguish, *me* is my desire.
Temptation, possession—all this confusion—it's your sense of *me*.

"Just utter the name of Hari, He is literally the 'Reliever'!
And He'll rob you of all your power, your pride and stiffness. Be
    One, with Heaven!

"The body perishes. It's just a bundle of five senses.
Blow it into the wind! After all, it's just air!"

Muktai gave Changa his lost life back.
She taught him how to have a home that's no property.

:DC

: NAMDEV
(1270—1350)

The night is black. The water pot is black.
Oh my mother!
The waters of the Yamuna
Are black too.

The veil is black. The jewel is black.
Oh my mother!
The pearls I wear around my neck
Are also black.

I am black. My breasts are clothed in black.
Oh my mother!
The waist-knot of my sari is
Also black.

The maiden lover
Goes alone to the river.
O my mother! Send her the black image of her lover
As company!

Nama, the servant of Vishnu,
Has a black mistress. Oh my mother!
How black can the image of Krishna
Be?

:DC

in the beginning
is the ant
mouth of the triple river
is the mouth of the ant

in darkness
is the ant
in flames a wick of water
lights a lamp of soot

in the wake
of the ant
all the sky follows

the world of our making's her droppings

i pursue
that ant
i, visnudas nama
unlock the ant with my guru

:AK

⁝ JANABAI
(1298—1350)

Jani sweeps with a broom
The Lord loads up the garbage

He carries it in a basket on His head
Throws it away in a distant dump

So much under the spell of Bhakti is He
He now performs the lowliest tasks

Says Jani to Vithoba
How shall I return Your favours?

:DC

Jani's head feels awfully itchy
Vithabai runs to help her feel easy

The Lord loosens the bun of her hair
Quickly picking out lice from there

He combs and brushes Jani's hair
I feel so clean says Jani

:DC

Jani loosens her hair
Among basil plants growing wild

The Lord with butter in the palm of His hand
Gently massages her head

My poor little Jani has no one but me
He thinks as he pours water on her head

Jani tells all the folks
My boyfriend gives me a shower

:DC

see the void
above the void
on its top
another void

the first void
is red
it's called
the lower void

the higher void
is white
the middle void
is grey

but the great void
is blue
it contains
only itself

jani was struck
with wonder
when she heard
the silent bell

:AK

i eat god
i drink god
i sleep
on god

i buy god
i count god
i deal
with god

god is here
god is there

void is not
devoid of god

    jani says:

god is within
god is without
and moreover
there's god to spare

    :AK

: Eknath

(1533—1599)

wonder of wonders
a thief stole a town
but when the trackers tracked him down
no thief, no town

the town was entirely unfounded
the temple windblown
god confounded
the steeple shot across heaven

the foundation fled
to the recesses of hell
and the wall wandered
from door to door

the foundation the wall the temple
underneath all paradox
the meaning is simple

:AK

⦂ TUKARAM
(1608 — 1650)

This is really extraordinary, O Hari,
You are supposed to relieve misery;
And here I am, your own devotee,
Whose house is haunted by poetry.

The more I excel in poems praising you,
The more my work seems flawed:
This is yet another amazing paradox.
Watchfulness is rewarded with anxiety.

Says Tuka, My Lord, it's just dawned on me:
To serve you is the ultimate difficulty.

⦂DC

Some of you may say
I am the author
Of these poems.
But
Believe me
This voice
Is not my own.

I have no
Personal skill.
It is
The Cosmic One
Making me speak.

What does a poor fellow like me
Know of the subtleties of meaning?
I speak what Govind
Makes me say.

He has appointed me
To measure it out.
The authority rests
With the Master; Not me.

Says Tuka, I'm only the servant.
See?
All this bears
The seal of His Name.

:DC

Advice to an Angry Wife

"Now there's nothing left for you to eat.
Will you eat your own children?
My husband is God-crazy!

"See how he beats his own head?
See how he wears garlands!
He has stopped minding his shop.

"His own belly is full
While the rest of us must starve

"Look at him striking cymbals
And opening his grotesque mouth
To sing to his God in his shrine!"

Says Tuka, be patient, my woman!
This is only the beginning!

:DC

Advice to an Angry Wife

"He can't stand the idea of work;
He is used to getting free meals.

"As soon as he wakes, he starts to sing.
All hell breaks loose after that.

"These fellows are the living dead.
They have no conscience to prick.

"They've turned a blind eye to their families.
They have deserted their homes.

"Their wives twist and turn for them
While they crush their lives with a stone."

Says Tuka, that's a good one, my wife!
Here! I've written it down!

:DC

In this Age of Evil poetry is an infidel's art:
The world teems with theatrical performers.

Their craving for money, lusting for women, and sheer reproduction
Define their values and priorities:
And what they mouth has no connection with their own being.

Hypocrites! They pretend such concern for where the world is
    going,
Talk of self-sacrifice, which is far from their minds.

They cite Vedic injunctions but can't do themselves any good.
They are unable to view their own bodies in perspective.

Says Tuka, a torturesome death awaits
All those whose language is divorced from being.

:DC

Without seeing a thing
I've seen entirely.
I've achieved a likeness
Of everybody.

Without taking
I've accepted.
My arms and legs
Are holidays.

Without eating
I've had my fill.
My mouth as it watered
Became the menu.

Without a word
I've spoken.
I've presented what
At best was absent.

The poem occurs,
Says Tuka,
Unknown
To my ears.

:AK

What will I eat now,
Where will I go?
Do I dare to stay on
In the village?

Villagers furious
Their chieftain grumpy,
If I beg I'll only see
The door in my face.

I'm shameless, they say,
An exhibitionist.
The elders in a conference
Are taking a decision.

The angry gentry
Have done their bit
And brought ruin
On a defenseless man.

What do I want, says Tuka,
With these people?
I must get going now
And search for Vithal.

:AK

The Varkaris

Each VARKARI POET of note claims a distinct story and a unique set of poems, yet the principal ones seem so closely aligned with one another—through kinship, household residence, or teacher-student descent—that it makes sense to treat them together. Often their biographies intertwine.

The word *varkari* means pilgrim or traveler, a term used for both a religious tradition of Maharashtra State and its poet-saints. The devoted Varkari hopes at least once in his or her life to make the pilgrimage to Pandharpur (or Pandhari) to visit the image of Vithoba (colloquially, Vithal), a deity who contains aspects of both Krishna and Śiva. The Vithoba images show the god standing on a brick. An early devotee had called upon Vithoba, but was busy when Vithoba arrived. The man provided a brick for the god to wait upon, then went off and forgot about him. Vithoba waited patiently, a long, long time, which endears him to his petitioners.

As holders of a subversive Hindu tradition, the Varkaris had numerous followers, making the poets social revolutionaries as much as spiritual guides or literary heroes. They openly denounced or made fun of the Brahmans' obscure rituals and slavish adherence to scripture. Varkaris treasure the songs of their poet-saints over Sanskrit texts.

Until the close of the seventeenth century the Varkaris remained the principal force in Marathi literature—the writing of Maharashtra State—and Dilip Chitre, their most dedicated modern translator, says they established the ground for the literature that would follow. So little did the poets care for status or hierarchy that even age set no authority. As a teenager Muktabai had an elderly hermit,

Changdev, for a student, and Janabai claimed intimate relations with Vithal though she was multiply dispossessed—an orphan, a woman, a servant, the follower of a heterodox tradition, and a religious poet singing not in Sanskrit but in her native tongue. Despite persecution, a trickster, extravagant, at times clownlike quality animates some of the poets. This reaches its height with Tukaram's poems to his wife.

JÑANDEV (1275—1296) Jñandev is best known for his Sanskrit-language *Jnaneshvari*, a commentary on the Bhagavad-gītā. He is considered the first of the Varkari poets, their "archmentor and preceptor," in Dilip Chitre's words. He composed his early work in Sanskrit, but then broke with orthodox convention and discarded the terms and the language of his priestly upbringing. Jñandev took to the language and folk meters of the nonliterate local people. The Varkaris who succeeded him all used vernacular language and also modeled poems on folk traditions.

Jñandev's father had been a disciple of a great celibate guru, Ramanand, but married and became a householder. Publicly shamed by Brahman authorities for this change of life, he and his wife were ostracized, hounded, and finally pressured into suicide. The Brahmans mocked and reviled the couple's four children: Nivrutti, Jñandev, Sopan, and their young sister Muktabai. That is, until the children proved spiritual accomplishments which dwarfed the realizations of their detractors. Though quite young, they took on the Brahmans in public debate and composed a series of treatises, including Jñandev's *Jnaneshvari,* that refuted the ideology of the Brahmans. They established what became the Varkaris' first tenet: God is not separate from the world in all its manifestations.

Jñandev drew on two folksong traditions. The first is the *ovi,* used by women working with mortar and pestle or at the *rahat,* a Persian-style water wheel. Most *ovi* lyrics are protest songs more than work songs—complaints about a life of grinding hard labor, grousings about unhappy marriages and despotic husbands, or sarcasm flung at the patriarchal family structure. Frequently the songs petition a deity to deliver the singer from servitude. The other model Jñandev took up was the *abhang*, a style of call-and-response used for religious ceremony, epic storytelling, and other social performances. Jñandev drew on stories of Krishna for his *abhang*-style poems. Along with the affectionate term Vithal for Vithoba, he used the names Hari and Govind, depicting his chosen deity as a "blue cowherd."

At age twenty-two Jñandev descended into an underground vault beneath the Vithoba temple at Alandi, near the modern city of Pune, and entered a trance, the *sanjeevan samādhi*, giving up worldly existence. He would have learnt from Nath yogins the technique of choosing one's point of departure from life.

MUKTABAI (1279—1297) Sister of Jñandev. Once when her older brother had been humiliated by Brahmans, fallen into despair, and sequestered himself in his room, Muktabai drew him out of his dark mood: "We Varkaris, no, we do not hide out from life." She took for a disciple the renowned, elderly yogin, Changdev, who regarded her as his "mother" and would sit in her lap. At age eighteen she vanished, consumed in a purple flash of lightning. Like her brother Jñandev, she may have learnt from Nath yogins the ability to choose one's method of departure from the world.

NAMDEV (1270—1350) Born into a tailor's family, he took Jñandev as his guru, though Jñandev was younger and of a higher caste. Once when Vithoba appeared in a dream, Namdev impulsively pledged to compose a billion poems of praise to the god. In order to meet the billion-poem vow, Namdev assigned large numbers to members of his household, including his mother and their servant girl Janabai.

JANABAI (1298—1350) Orphaned early, she worked in Namdev's house. It is hard to tell if she regarded the higher-caste poet as a guru or simply someone she worked for. She directed a good deal of venom at Namdev's mother, who following tradition would have run the household. Janabai's poetry complains about the bitter work she has to accept as a low-caste servant from employers who stand only a bit higher in the social order. Yet she shows rapture, and deep gratification at the help she receives from Vithal, who shows up to help her with the most demeaning chores. Vithal grooms her, too, something women do for each other, not gods.

Also strange—to the Brahmans this would have seemed the final indignity—Janabai sometimes adds -*bai*, sister, to the god's name. "Vithalabai." As though he's a girlfriend.

EKNATH (1533—1599) At a time when Brahmans avoided the shadows and even the voices of untouchables, the scholar and poet Eknath showed respect and sought their company. "Every soul you encounter is god," says one of his songs. Poetry of the earlier Varkaris had mostly disappeared over the two previous centuries, due to continual raids by Muslim armies. Eknath became obsessed with Jñandev and located the poet's tomb, proving to a dispirited Marathi people that Jñandev was no legend but a figure of national pride. He labored for years to restore Jñandev's writings. Then, following his hero, Eknath chose his own death-illumination, *jal samādhi*, submerging himself in the Godavari River.

TUKARAM (1608—1650) The best-known poet of the Varkaris. Little about Tuka's life can be verified, but the circulating stories show how deep he sits in popular imagination. Since he was born a śudra, at the bottom of the caste hierarchy, no one should expect much documented biography, though.

Despite his low birth, the stories show Tuka as a prosperous, civic-minded, properly devout businessman. He may have inherited family property, and held a sizable estate, with enough land to build a temple. This Rotary Club life changed when Namdev and Eknath—two predecessors, dead centuries before Tuka was born—visited him in a dream. In the dream Namdev assigned Tuka a large number of devotional poems to write—to help with the billion Namdev himself had pledged to Vithoba three hundred years earlier. From that point on Tuka had only one desire: to praise his god in poetry. To complete the assignment—and out of spiritual convictions that left little room for commercial dealings or family affairs—Tukaram let his shop, his business, and his family estate fall into disrepair. A few poems laced with grim, self-effacing humor show him parrying with his wife. Tuka can sound victimized by his devotion, beginning with the dream in which Namdev commands him to write poems.

That Tukaram would write religious poems, and do it in Marathi, not Sanskrit, outraged the Brahmans, who thought no *śudra* should even speak on religious matters. Dilip Chitre writes, "He was eventually forced to throw his manuscripts into the local Indrayani River at Dehu, his native village, and was presumably told by his mocking detractors that if indeed he were a true devotee of God, then God would restore his sunken notebooks." Tukaram sat by the riverside, praying and fasting; thirteen days later his notebooks of poetry surfaced, undamaged by water. The notebooks were conserved in a nearby temple.

Not long after his poetry came back, Tuka disappeared. A few late poems take the form of last words of counsel to friends or followers, written before he walked out of town and vanished into the unknown. He seems to have disappeared without trace. Whispers and rumors go around, though: What if Tuka did not set out on pilgrimage? What if hostile religious officers did away with him?

: AKHO (AKHA BHAGAT)
(1591—1656)

Turban tilted rakishly
    to hide the bald spot,
    but how will that mask
    the emptiness in your heart?

Such dandy twirled whiskers,
    such fancy tripping speech!
    Fool, Death tomorrow
    thumps on a slackened drum.

Your charade goes poof,
    a miserable fart.
    Akha says: Rotted doors
    fall apart.

His acquaintance with Hari—nil!
    But he sits decked in ochre,
    guru's garb pulled out
    from some bag of tricks.

As snake goes visiting fellow reptile's den,
    disciples saunter in
    to exchange a lick on the mouth with him,
    before they slither homeward again.

There are too many such gurus in the world!
    Small chance, says Akha,
    they give you a hand
    to reach you across.

:GP

Where the creature is
   there is the Creator,
   but you wander elsewhere,
   search in faraway places.

The first false step, says Akha,
   was that you forgot
   to look within.

So you forgot.
   Go then, study
   with a saint. What's gained
   by shows of piety:
   one day all whiskers and beard,
   the next day tonsured, sheared?

:GP

The Dude! Bathed, scrubbed,
　　perfumed, tucking in
　　eats till he bloats
　　stud size.

Battening on
　　each pleasure on earth,
　　a germ of Maya sits crouching
　　in that bulk.

That carcass
　　believes Maya to be his friend.
　　Maya will chew him down
　　to his entrails.

:GP

Akho

AKHA BHAGAT, affectionately called Akho, lived in what is today Gujarat State. Born in 1591 in the village of Jetalpur, he moved nearby, to the city of Ahmedabad. A goldsmith by caste and profession—considered low-caste and magically impure due to contact with chemicals—his reputation rests on his six-line *chhappa*s or poem-sayings. In them he savages the caste system, calls out religious hypocrisy where he sees it, and displays intense revulsion for religious rituals used to exclude the poor or the vulnerable. Available facts about his life are scant. He suffered the deaths of both parents, his only sister, and two wives, which may mark his poetry with a dark outlook. Portraits show a turbaned figure with huge moustache falling over a grim mouth, a prominent ring in his ear, and a demeanor seasoned with hard thought. He wrote perhaps 746 terse, pointed *chhappa*s, along with a number of longer philosophical poems. Based on his work, it is evident he had a hunger for learning; his poetry shows knowledge of Hindu scripture, astrology, astronomy, medicine, music, sculpture, and agriculture. He was informed about the properties of minerals and plants and the habits of birds and animals, and he distinguishes auspicious from inauspicious days based on astrological calculation.

Akho died in 1656. The quarters he held in Ahmedabad, popularly known as *Akha no Ordo* or Akha's Room, became over the years a pilgrim destination. In 2005 a historical organization of Ahmedabad restored them, setting a bronze likeness of him in the courtyard. The city's 2012 Heritage Festival honors Akho prominently on its website; yet this principal literary figure of Gujarat remains virtually unknown to those who do not speak Gujarati. This is ironic: Gujarat State has sixty million citizens—a population larger than the country of England.

: KABIR
(1398—1448)

Certain Poems of Kabir
From the English versions of Kali Mohan Ghose

I

The spring season is approaching,
Who will help me meeting with my dearest?
How shall I describe the beauty of the dearest,
Who is immersed in all beauties?
That color colors all the pictures of this universe,
Body and mind alike
Forget all things else in that beauty.
He who has these ideas,
The play of the spring is his.
This is the word which is unutterable.
Saith Kabir: There are very few who know this mystery.

II

My beloved is awakened, how can I sleep?
Day and night he is calling me,
And instead of responding to his call
I am like an unchaste girl, living with another.
Saith Kabir: O clever confidant,
The meeting with the dearest is not possible without love.

III

The scar aches day and night.
Sleep is not come.

Anxious for meeting with the dearest,
The father's house is not attractive at all.
The sky-gate opens,
The temple is manifested,
There now is the meeting with the husband.
I make oblation of my mind and body:
To the dearest the cup of the dearest!
Let flow the quick shower of rain from your eyes.
Cover your heart
With the intense deep blue
Assembling of the cloud.
Come near to the ear of the dearest,
Whisper to him your pain.
Saith Kabir: Here bring the meditation of the dearest,
Today's treasure of the heart.

IV

It is true, I am mad with love. And what to me
Is carefulness or uncarefulness?
Who, dying, wandering in the wilderness,
Who is separated from the dearest?
My dearest is within me, what do I care?
The beloved is not asundered from me,
No, not for the veriest moment.
And I also am not asundered from him.
My love clings to him only,
Where is restlessness in me?
Oh my mind dances with joy,
Dances like a mad fool.
The raginis of love are being played day and night,
All are listening to that measure.
Rahu, the eclipse, Ketu, the Head of the Dragon,
And the nine planets are dancing,

And birth and death are dancing, mad with Ananda.
The mountain, the sea and the earth are dancing,
The Great Adornment is dancing with laughter and tears and
    smiles.
Why are you leaving "the world,"
You with the *tilak*-mark on your forehead?
While my mind is a-dancing through the thousand stages of its
    moon,
And the Lord of all his creation has found it acceptable dancing.

    V
O deserted bride,
How will you live in the absence of your beloved,
Without hunger in the day,
Sleepless in the night watches,
And every watch felt as if
It were the aeon of Kaliyuga?
The beautiful has deserted you in the full passion of his April.
Alas the fair is departed!
O Thou deserted,
Now begin to give up your house and your having.
Go forth to the lodge of the forest,
Begin to consider his name.
And if there he shall come upon you,
Then alone will you be come to your joy.
Eager as the caught fish for its water,
Be thou so eager to return!
Shapeless, formless and without line,
Who will be come to meet you,
O beautiful lady?
Take recognizance of your own wed Lord,
Behold him out of the center of your meditations,
Strip off the last of your errors,

And know that Love is your lord.
Saith Kabir: There is no second. Aeon
After aeon
Thou and I are the same.

VI

Very difficult is the meeting with him,
How shall I be made one with my beloved?
After long consideration and after caution
I put my feet on the way, but every time
They have trembled and slipped aside.
The slippery path leads upward and the feet cannot hold to it.
The mind is taken in shyness,
For fear of the crowd
And out of respect to the family.
Oh where is my far beloved?
And I in the family dwelling!
And I can not escape my shyness!

VII

How shall it be severed,
This love between thee and me?
Thou art lord, and I servant,
As the lotus is servant of water.
Thou art lord, and I servant,
As the Chakora is servant of the moonlight
And watches it all the night long.
The love between thee and me is from beginning to ending,
How can it end in time?
Saith Kabir: As the river is immersed in the ocean,
My mind is immersed in thee.

VIII

Rishi Narad, that hast walked upon the winding path of the air,
That has walked there playing the Vina and singing thy song to
    Hari,
Rishi Narad, the beloved is not afar off,
I wake not, save in his waking,
I sleep not, save in his slumber.

IX

O receiver of my heart,
Do thou come into my house,
My mind and body
Are but a pain, in thy absence.
When they say that I am your mistress
The shame of it is upon me.
If heart lie not upon heart,
How is the heart of love there?
The rice has no savor, the night is passed and is sleepless.
In the house and in the way of the forest my mind and
    thought have no rest.
Love-cup to the maid: water-cup to famished of thirst,
is there one, bearer of fortune, to make clear my heart to my
    beloved?
Kabir is at the end of his patience
And dies without sight of his beloved.

X

O bearer of love, give voice to the well-omened song.
The great lord is come to my house.
After employing my body in his love
I shall employ my mind.
The five mysteries will be enlightened with love.
The receiver of my heart, today is the guest in my house,

I am grown mad with my youth.
The pool of my body will be the place of pilgrimage.
Near by will Brahman chant Vedas,
The mind will be fused with my lover.

O opportune, and well-omened,
The three and thirty tunes of curious sound here with the
    sound of Ananda.
The paired lovers of the universe are assembled.
Saith Kabir: This day I set out for my marriage
With a bridegroom who is deathless.
In the quarter of my body there is music in process,
Thirty and six raginis are bound up into the burthen.
The bridegroom hath April play with me.
As Krishna with Radha, playing at the spring festival of Harilila,
I play at the spraying of colors, I and my beloved.
The whole universe is curious today.
Love and the rain of love are come hither with their showers.

:EP

The gardener's wife
Cuts short the brief life
Of the flowers and offers them
To a lifeless stone idol
That a sculptor carved,
Feet on its chest,
Chisel in hand.

Had the idol been alive,
It would have
Lashed out at the sculptor.
It would have seen through the priest
Who grabs all the food
The faithful bring,
Leaving the scraps to the idol.

Not one, not two,
But everyone's a sucker,
Says Kabir. Not me.

:AKM

Kabir has dismantled
His loom
And on his body he has inscribed
Rama's name.

His mother
Is too distraught to speak.
How, she keeps asking,
Will he make ends meet?

He wants to tell her
He can't thread the shuttle,
Not anymore, now that Rama's
Love is the thread in his hand.

But Mother, says Kabir,
Listen. The lord
Of three worlds is our protector.
He won't let us starve.

:AKM

Easy friend,
What's the big fuss about?

Once dead,
The body that was stuffed with
Kilos of sweets
Is carried out to be burnt,
And the head on which
A bright turban was tied
Is rolled by crows in the dust.
A man with a stick
Will poke the cold ashes
For your bones.

But I'm wasting my time,
Says Kabir,
Even death's bludgeon
About to crush your head
Won't wake you up.

:AKM

Think twice before you keep
The bad company
Of someone like me.

The bitter neem that keeps
The bad company
Of a sandalwood tree
Begins to smell like sandalwood.

The piece of iron that keeps
The bad company
Of the philosopher's stone
Turns into gold.

Waters that drain
Into the Ganges
Become the Ganges.

And those who keep
The bad company
Of Rama, says Kabir,
End up

A bit like Rama.

:AKM

Except that it robs you of who you are,
What can you say about speech?
Inconceivable to live without
And impossible to live with,
Speech diminishes you.
Speak with a wise man, there'll be
Much to learn; speak with a fool,
All you get is prattle.
Strike a half-empty pot, and it'll make
A loud sound; strike one that is full,
Says Kabir, and hear the silence.

:AKM

Brother, I've seen some
    Astonishing sights:
A lion keeping watch
    Over pasturing cows;
A mother delivered
    After her son was;
A guru prostrated
    Before his disciple;
Fish spawning
    On treetops;
A cat carrying away
    A dog;
A gunnysack
    Driving a bullock cart;
A buffalo gone out to graze,
    Sitting on a horse;
A tree with its branches in the earth,
    Its roots in the sky;
A tree with flowering roots.

This verse, says Kabir,
    Is your key to the universe.
If you can figure it out.

:AKM

Sākhīs *

Why is the doe thin
by the green
pool? One deer,
a hundred thousand
hunters. How to escape
the spear?

. . . .

Kabir's house is at the top
of a narrow, slippery track.
An ant's foot
won't fit.
So, villain,
why load your bullock?

. . . .

* The short verse of Kabir and various contemporaries, typically written in two
lines, is popularly called a *sākhī*. The word derives from Sanskrit, *sākṣī*, "with the
eyes." *Eyewitness* might be a good translation, as the poems testify to something
the poet has encountered or met in his or her own life. These testimonies are not
hearsay, not old wisdom, but speak to direct experience.
    Since Kabir may not have known how to read or write, the notion of "two lines"
could well have been alien to him. He would have heard syllabic rhythms or musi-
cal phrases.

Gorakh was yoga's connoisseur.
They didn't cremate
his body.
Still his meat rotted and mixed
with dust. For nothing
he polished his body.

· · · · · · · · · · ·

Into the looking-glass cavern
the dog goes running.
Seeing his own reflection,
he dies barking.

· · · · · · · · · ·

Homage to the milk
that yields butter.
In half a couplet of Kabir's
the life
of the four Vedas.

· · · · · · · · · ·

On this riverbank, saints or thieves?
You'll know as soon as they talk.
The character deep within
comes out by the road of the mouth.

· · · · · · · · · ·

In the wood where lions
don't tread
and birds don't fly,
Kabir ranges
in empty meditation.

:LH & SS

The true guru went out hunting,
a red bow in his hand.
Many fools escaped,
Now and then, a true seeker was hit.

. . . .

When I was here, God was gone.
Now God is here, I'm gone.
The lane of love is very narrow.
Two can't go in.

. . . .

Slowly, slowly, oh mind,
everything happens slowly.
The gardener pours hundreds of jars
of water
but fruit comes
only in season.

:LH

When you die, what do you do with your body?
Once the breath stops
you have to put it away.
There are several ways to deal
with spoiled flesh.
Some burn it, some bury it
in the ground.
Hindus prefer cremation,
Turks burial.
But in the end, one way or another,
both have to leave home.
Death spreads the karmic net
like a fisherman snaring fish.
What is a man without Ram?
Kabir says, you'll be sorry later
when you go from this house
to that one.

Saints, I see the world is mad.
If I tell the truth they rush to beat me,
if I lie they trust me.
I've seen the pious Hindus, rule-followers,
early morning bath-takers—
killing souls, they worship rocks.
They know nothing.
I've seen plenty of Muslim teachers, holy men
reading their holy books
and teaching their pupils techniques.
They know just as much.
And posturing yogis, hypocrites,
hearts crammed with pride,
praying to brass, to stones, reeling
with pride in their pilgrimage,
fixing their caps and their prayer-beads,
painting their brow-marks and arm-marks,
braying their hymns and their couplets,
reeling. They never heard of soul.
The Hindu says Ram is the Beloved,
the Turk says Rahim.
Then they kill each other.
No one knows the secret.
They buzz their mantras from house to house,
puffed with pride.
The pupils drown along with their gurus.
In the end they're sorry.
Kabir says, listen saints:
they're all deluded!
Whatever I say, nobody gets it.
It's too simple.

:LH & SS

She went with her husband to the in-laws' house
but didn't sleep with him,
didn't enjoy him.
Her youth slipped away like a dream.
Four met and fixed the marriage date,
five came and fixed the canopy,
girlfriends sang the wedding songs
and rubbed on her brow the yellow paste
of joy and sorrow.
Through many forms her mind turned
as she circled the fire.
The knot was tied, the pledge was made,
the married women poured the water.
Yet with her husband on the wedding square
she became a widow.
She left her marriage without the groom.
On the road the father-in-law explained.
Kabir says, I'm off to my real marriage now.
I'll play the trumpet
when I cross with my lord.

:LH & SS

Friend, wake up! Why do you go on sleeping?
The night is over—do you want to lose the day
    the same way?
Other women who managed to get up early have
    already found an elephant or a jewel. . . .
So much was lost already while you slept. . . .
and that was so unnecessary!

The one who loves you understood, but you did not.
You forgot to make a place in your bed next to you.
Instead you spent your life playing.
In your twenties you did not grow
because you did not know who your Lord was.
Wake up! Wake up! There's no one in your bed—
He left you during the night.

Kabir says: The only woman awake is the woman
    who has heard the flute!

: RB

To whom shall I go to learn about the one I love?
Kabir says: "When you're trying to find a hardwood forest,
    it seems wise to know what a tree is.
If you want to find the Lord, please forget about abstract nouns."

I played for ten years with the girls my own age,
    but now I am suddenly in fear.
I am on the way up some stairs—they are high.
Yet I have to give up my fears
if I want to take part in this love.

I have to let go the protective clothes
and meet him with the whole length of my body.
My eyes will have to be the love-candles this time.
Kabir says: Men and women in love will understand
    this poem.
If what you feel for the Holy One is not desire,
then what's the use of dressing with such care,
and spending so much time making your eyelids
    dark?

:RB

There is nothing but water in the holy pools.
I know, I have been swimming in them.
All the gods sculpted of wood or ivory can't say a word.
I know, I have been crying out to them.
The Sacred Books of the East are nothing but words.
I looked through their covers one day sideways.
What Kabir talks of is only what he has lived
    through.
If you have not lived through something, it is not
    true.

:RB

Kabir

K ABIR WAS BORN in the city of Varanasi (Benares) in 1398 to a family of Muslim weavers. Beyond this detail, little about his life can be verified. Facts lie buried in a huge body of legend that has accrued around Kabir, tales that reveal a poet of uncompromising honesty, a singer so confrontational that he stands unique in history, a man who displays a wily, trickster personality. He is a "coyote" of poetry, ruthlessly unpredictable, full of shivery ambiguity, who skewers every deluded notion about life or death. In his wake he left a set of teachings, or an attitude toward the world, claimed by Hindus, Sikhs, Muslims, and poets. Several religious sects use his poetry for scripture. His admirers can stand at odds with each other but all agree on his formidable stature.

Kabir's teacher is reputed to have been the celebrated Hindu yogin Ramanand. As a young man Kabir sought Ramanand out, hoping to take the older man as his guru. But Ramanand could not accept Kabir as a student; a Muslim would have violated Hindu rules of purity or propriety by his presence. So Kabir set a trap. He rose in the predawn dark one morning, and hustled down to a spot he knew Ramanand walked past every day on his way to early ablutions and prayers by the Ganges River. In Varanasi you approach the river by descending its ancient ghats, great granite steps and platforms that drop steeply from the city's narrow winding streets to the waters. Some platforms serve for cremation; others are frequented by worshippers, pilgrims, yoga practitioners, scholars, boatmen, children, dogs, and in modern times tourists. The devout descend them mornings before dawn.

Kabir lay on the steps in the darkness, directly in the course Ramanand took. Stepping down the angular stones, the great teacher stumbled over Kabir in the misty, leaden twilight. In shock or fear he cried out his personal mantra: "Ram, Ram. Ram, Ram." Standing up, Kabir declared that Ramanand had just transmitted a powerful, personal mantra to him. By longstanding tradition, Ramanand was now required to accept Kabir as a student.

Most of what passes for fact about Kabir's life comes from his poems. One *sākhī* suggests he could have been illiterate.

> I don't touch ink or paper,
> this hand never grasped a pen.
> The greatness of the four ages
> Kabir tells with his mouth alone.
> (LH & SS translation)

Another *sākhī* makes it clear that his razor-toothed poems drew hostility, probably from both Brahmans and Muslims:

> If I speak out I'm beaten.
> When the veil's up, no one sees.
> The dog hides under the haystack.
> Why talk and make enemies?
> (LH & SS translation)

One stanza draws speculation: "I speak the language of the East. People of the West don't comprehend me." This could say something about his dialect—which scholars can't quite make out—or does it refer to a symbolic or initiatory language? Secret languages, tongues hidden within tongues or words veiled in words, have a long history in India. Texts and oral teachings of Tantra will cultivate the reflection, the echo, the cipher; symbols and riddles show up in the religious sects of the era; Kabir could have trained in one or more of these traditions. A term that circulated in his day, *ulaṭbāṃsī*, means "upside-down speech": a language deliberately coded. Most of the poems speak with reckless honesty, though. Nobody needs a code book to get

> I've burnt my own
> house down
> the torch is in my hands—
> now I'll burn down the house
> of anyone
> who wants to follow me.
> (AS translation)

As with many North Indian poets, Kabir's work comes to the modern world in two ways. First it exists as oral poetry, sung in the streets, temples, bazaars, and fields, as well as on the concert hall stage. We also receive it as written texts. Three main literary traditions have conserved his poems: the Guru Granth of the Sikhs in the Punjab, the Pancavani of the Dadu Panth from Rajasthan, and the Kabir Panth of Eastern India, for whom a Kabir collection called the Bijak is scripture.

The French scholar Charlotte Vaudeville has distinguished a "western tradition" of Kabir—those of the Sikhs and the Dadu Panth —from an eastern tradition. Notice how different Ezra Pound's translations are from Linda Hess's. The eastern tradition—the poems of the Bijak—comes off fiercer, more confrontational, and holds an uncompromising poetry nearly unique in its inventiveness. Of the western Kabir, Linda Hess writes that it is "a softer, more emotional Kabir who sings of ecstatic insight, who experiences passionate longing for and tormented separation from a beloved, or who offers himself in utter surrender, as a servant or beggar, to a personified divine master. Often the western poet's expressions are colored by the terms and forms of the Krishna *bhakti* (devotional) movement."

Miracles attended Kabir when alive, and followed him into death. At his funeral a group of Hindus and another of Muslims claimed his remains. The Hindus wanted to cremate him, following their tradition. The Muslims insisted they get his corpse and take it for burial. While Kabir's carcass lay under a shroud the two groups went from argument to blows. In the scuffle, several people fell and jolted the shroud back. Where Kabir's corpse had been resting was only a vast heap of marigolds. The two groups divided the flowers, the Hindus burning theirs, the Muslims carting the other half off to their cemetery.

Besides the eastern and western traditions of Kabir there exists for readers of English a third that juts out at an odd angle. This comes from a manuscript that emerged in Bengal in the nineteenth century—poems collected orally by a friend of Rabindranath Tagore. Tagore and Evelyn Underhill, an English writer and pacifist, together translated a hundred poems. Their book has been in print for a century, though the translations read poorly to modern ears. Robert Bly reworked about half of Tagore's versions into colloquial American English. This third Kabir, Tagore's and Bly's (who often sounds like a Sufi), holds a special place. It is the "east meets west" Kabir, a living presence in England and North America these past hundred years.

: Mirabai
(1498—1550)

Sister, the Dark One won't speak to me.
Why does this useless body keep breathing?
Another night gone
and no one's lifted my gown.
He won't speak to me.
Years pass, not a gesture.
They told me
he'd come when the rains came,
but lightning pierces the clouds,
the clock ticks until daybreak
and I feel the old dread.
Slave to the Dark One,
Mira's whole life is a long
night of craving.

:AS

He has stained me,
the color of raven he's stained me.
Beating a clay
two-headed drum at both ends
like a nautch girl I dance
before sadhus.
Back in town I'm called crazy,
drunkard, a love slut—
they incited the prince
who ordered me poisoned
but I drained the cup without missing a step.
Mira's lord is the true prince,
he stained her the color of raven,
birth after birth
she is his.

:AS

O Mind,
praise the lotus feet that don't perish!
Consider all things
on heaven and earth—and their doom.
Go off with pilgrims, undertake fasts,
wrangle for wisdom,
trek to Banaras to die,
what's the use?
Arrogant body just withers,
phenomenal world is a coy parakeet
that flies off at dusk.
Why throw a hermit robe over your shoulders—
yellow rag yogins
are also bewildered,
caught every time in the birth snare.
Dark One, take this girl for your servant.
Then cut the cords and
set her free.

:AS

You pressed Mira's seal of love
then walked out.
Unable to see you
she's hopeless,
tossing in bed—gasping her life out.
Dark One, it's your fault—
I'll join the yoginis,
I'll take a blade to my throat in Banaras.
Mira gave herself to you,
you touched her intimate seal
and then left.

:AS

How bitter is carnival day
with my lover off traveling.
O desolate town,
night and day wretched,
my small bed in the attic lies empty.
Rejected and lost
in his absence, stumbling under
the pain.
Must you wander
from country to country? It hurts me.
These fingers ache
counting the days you've been gone.
Spring arrives
with its festival games,
the chiming of anklets, drumbeats and flute, a sitar—
yet no beloved visits my gate.
What makes you forget?
Here I stand begging you, Dark One
don't shame me!
Mira comes to embrace you
birth after birth
   still a virgin.

:AS

Over the trees
a crescent moon glides.
The Dark One has gone to dwell in Mathura.
Me, I struggle, caught in a love noose
and yes,
Mira's lord can lift mountains
but today his passion
   seems distant and faint.

:AS

The Dark One's love-stain
is on her,
other ornaments
Mira sees as mere glitter.
A mark on her forehead,
a bracelet, some prayer beads,
beyond that she wears only
    her conduct.

Make-up is worthless
when you've gotten truth from a teacher.
O the Dark One has
stained me with love,
and for that some revile me,
others give honor.
I simply wander the road of the sadhus
    lost in my songs.

Never stealing,
injuring no one,
who can discredit me?
Do you think I'd step down from an elephant
to ride on the haunch
    of an ass?

:AS

The plums tasted
sweet to the unlettered desert-tribe girl,
but what manners! To chew into each!
She was ungainly,
low-caste, ill mannered and dirty,
but the god took the
fruit she'd been sucking.
Why? She knew how to love.
She might not distinguish
splendor from filth
but she'd tasted the nectar of passion.
Might not know any Veda,
but a chariot swept her away.
Now she frolics in heaven, passionately bound to her god.
The Lord of Fallen Fools, says Mira,
will save anyone
who can practice rapture like that.
I myself in a previous birth
was a cow-herding girl
at Gokul.

:AS

Dark One,
how can I sleep?
Since you left my bed
the seconds drag past like epochs,
each moment
a new torrent of pain.
I am no wife,
no lover comes through the darkness—
lamps, houses, no comfort.
On my couch
the embroidered flowers
pierce me like thistles,
    I toss through the night.

Yet who would believe my story?
That a lover
bit my hand like a snake,
and the venom bursts through
    and I'm dying?

I hear
the peacock's faraway gospel,
the nightingale's love song,
the cuckoo—
thickness on thickness folds through the sky,
clouds flash with rain.
Dark One, is there no love
in this world
that such anguish continues?
Mirabai waits for a
    glance from your eye.

∶AS

Yogin, don't go—
at your feet a slave girl has fallen.
She lost herself
on the devious path of romance and worship,
no one to guide her.
Now she's built
an incense and sandalwood pyre
and begs you to light it.
Dark One, don't go—
when only cinder remains
rub my ash over your body.
Mira asks, Dark One,
    can flame twist upon flame?

:AS

The song of the flute, O sister, is madness.
I thought that nothing that was not God could hold me,
But hearing that sound, I lose mind and body,
My heart wholly caught in the net.
O flute, what were your vows, what is your practice?
What power sits by your side?
Even Mira's Lord is trapped in your seven notes.

:JH

Love has stained my body
to the color of the One Who Holds Up Mountains.
When I dressed in the world's five fabrics,
I only played hide and seek—
For disguised though I was, the Lifting One caught me.
And seeing his beauty, I offered him all that I am.
Friends, let those whose Beloved is absent write letters—
Mine dwells in the heart, and neither enters nor leaves.
Mira has given herself to her Lord Giridhara.
Day or night, she waits only for him.

:JH

O my friends,
What can you tell me of Love,
Whose pathways are filled with strangeness?
When you offer the Great One your love,
At the first step your body is crushed.
Next be ready to offer your head as his seat.
Be ready to orbit his lamp like a moth giving in to the light,
To live in the deer as she runs toward the hunter's call,
In the partridge that swallows hot coals for love of the moon,
In the fish that, kept from the sea, happily dies.
Like a bee trapped for life in the closing of the sweet flower,
Mira has offered herself to her Lord.
She says, the single Lotus will swallow you whole.

:JH

Awake to the Name

To be born in a human body is rare,
Don't throw away the reward of your past good deeds.
Life passes in an instant—the leaf doesn't go back to the branch.
The ocean of rebirth sweeps up all beings hard,
Pulls them into its cold-running, fierce, implacable currents.
Giridhara, your name is the raft, the one safe-passage over.
Take me quickly.
All the awake ones travel with Mira, singing the name.
She says with them: Get up, stop sleeping—the days of a life
    are short.

:JH

The Coffer with the Poisonous Snake

Rana sent a gold coffer of complicated ivory;
But inside a black and green asp was waiting,
"It is a necklace that belonged to a great Queen!"
I put it around my neck; it fit well.
It became a string of lovely pearls, each with a moon inside.
My room then was full of moonlight, as if the full moon
Had found its way in through the open window.

:RB

The Clouds

When I saw the dark clouds, I wept, O Dark One,
    I wept at the dark clouds.
Black clouds soared up, and took some yellow along;
    rain did fall, some rain fell long.
There was water east of the house, west of the house;
    fields all green.
The one I love lives past those fields; rain has fallen
    on my body, on my hair, as I wait in the open
    door for him.
The Energy that holds up mountains is the energy
    Mirabai bows down to.
He lives century after century, and the test I set for
    him he has passed.

:RB

All I Was Doing Was Breathing

Something has reached out and taken in the beams of my eyes.
There is a longing, it is for his body, for every hair of that dark body.
All I was doing was being, and the Dancing Energy came by my
   house.
His face looks curiously like the moon, I saw it from the side,
   smiling.
My family says: "Don't ever see him again!" And they imply things
   in a low voice.
But my eyes have their own life; they laugh at rules, and know
   whose they are.
I believe I can bear on my shoulders whatever you want to say of me.
Mira says: Without the energy that lifts mountains, how am I to
   live?

:RB

The Heat of Midnight Tears

Listen, my friend, this road is the heart opening,
Kissing his feet, resistance broken, tears all night.

If we could reach the Lord through immersion in water,
I would have asked to be born a fish in this life.
If we could reach him through nothing but berries and wild nuts
Then surely the saints would have been monkeys when they came
    from the womb!
If we could reach him by munching lettuce and dry leaves
Then the goats would surely get to the Holy One before us!

If the worship of stone statues could bring us all the way,
I would have adored a granite mountain years ago.

Mirabai says: The heat of midnight tears will bring you to God.

:RB

Mirabai

THE FIRST ACCOUNT of Mirabai's life comes from the *Bhak-tamāla* of Nabhadas, a hagiography of North Indian bhakti saints composed around 1600 CE, not long after Mira's death. It shows how close to her own lifetime she had fired the imagination:

> Mira shattered the manacles
> of civility, family, and shame.
> A latter day *gopi*, she made love explicit
> for the dark Kali Yuga.
> Independent, unutterably fearless,
> she sang her delight for an
> amorous god.
> Scoundrels thought her a dangerous presence
> and ventured to kill her,
> but draining like nectar the poison they sent
> she stepped forth unscathed.
> Striking the drumskin of devotion
> Mira cringed before no one.
> Family, civility, gossip —
> she shattered the manacles.
> She sang praise to her lord the
> lifter of mountains.
> (AS translation)

Mira was born into a Rajput clan, the Rathors, who ruled the city of Merta, Rajasthan, and its surrounding villages. Her warrior family married her into a substantial nearby clan, the Sisodia Rajputs of

Mewar, in an effort to establish a military alliance. But the girl quickly alienated her powerful in-laws. By the Rajput institution of *suhag*, her religious duties were to be discharged in unquestioning service to her husband. However, from an early age she believed herself betrothed to Krishna and refused to abide by secular custom. One account says she dutifully touched her mother-in-law's feet but swept past their image of Kali, the dark goddess, saying she'd long been on most intimate terms with the true Lord, and could not bow to a lump of stone.

Some say her husband was weak-minded, unable or unwilling to force her compliance. It's thought that he perished on the field of battle shortly after their marriage. All the stories agree, though: Mira had refused intimacy with him—her true husband was Śyām, the "Dark One," Krishna. As an infant, Mira may have gotten "a true word" from a wandering holy man who whispered briefly into her ear. She now claimed to have been born through the ages—in one song, she has dropped from 84,000 wombs—to love only Śyām. Despite her husband's death she refused the clothes of a widow, would not sequester herself, and rejected the conventions of widowhood. Instead she often descended from the Sisodia palace to visit local temples where she consorted with sadhus, wandering mendicants, singing and dancing in worship of Śyām.

Her husband's family was outraged. The prince, or Rana, she refers to in many songs—probably her brother-in-law—both hated and feared her. The stories say he made three attempts on her life, aided by Mira's mother-in-law. Initially they sent poisoned water, claiming it to be *caranāmṛt*—holy water used to wash the feet of a Krishna image. In one of her most famous songs, Mira claims that as she danced she "drained the cup without missing a step."

A second attempt failed as well. The conspirators sent a snake in a basket of fruit, or in a jeweled coffer. When Mira lifted the lid of the basket or box the poisonous asp had turned into a *śālgrām*, the black fossil ammonite considered all over India to be a manifestation of Krishna.

After a third attempt on her life—palace guards forced her to lie on a bed of iron spikes, but her god turned them to flower petals—Mira fled the palace. All along she'd insisted her true family was the *sadhu sang*, the company of truth seekers. Now she ran from her life of privilege like a convict going over the wall—a suffocating life of wealth, status, power, luxury, female submission, and royal expectations. For the rest of her life she moved among the family of *bhakta*s, traveling the roads of North India on a perpetual search for her Giridhara-nāgara, the elegant one—the energy—that lifts mountains.

No manuscripts of Mirabai's poems survive from within two centuries of her death. Contemporary musicians think she sang her songs as she roamed. A loyal maid, Lalita, who had abandoned the palace with Mira and joined her on the road, transcribed the words into a great notebook, possibly noting down a raga for each song. Records from the Ranchhodji Temple at Dwarka refer to this notebook or a copy, but sometime in the seventeenth century a Muslim warlord plundered the temple and the manuscript vanished. For nearly five hundred years musicians have passed her songs on orally.

Modern collectors have located well over five thousand songs with the name Mirabai in the signature line. Scholars have tried to establish which might justifiably be thought hers, using linguistic evidence, and the popular *Padāvali* or edition of songs holds just over two hundred.

By the age of fifty Mira had arrived at the great Ranchhodji Temple at Dwarka, in Gujarat State, where she set up a kitchen to feed the poor. Around that time her husband's family, long absent from her life, decided they wanted their princess home. Their motives were likely political. They had suffered a series of punishing military setbacks, and persistent rumors went through the countryside that their vicious treatment of Mira had turned the favor of the gods. So they dispatched an envoy of Brahmans to Dwarka to fetch her.

At first Mira refused to return with the envoy. But the Brahmans vowed to fast to death if she wouldn't relent. This put her in a bind: If a Brahman should die on her account, the karma of his death would pursue her. Reluctantly, she agreed to return to Mewar. Before setting out, she asked for a final night alone in the temple with the image of Krishna. In the morning she did not emerge. The envoy forced open the temple doors, and found only Mira's hair and her robe slung across the lap of the deity.

A modern biographer notes that behind the temple lies the ocean. Mirabai could have left through a rear passage, climbed into a waiting boat, and slipped off across the water.

: SURDĀS

(1478—1583?)

To what land has Krishna departed?
I'll find him,
I'll go out in drag
with a bowl and an antler,
I'll be a saffron-robed, ash-pasted
beggar yoginī.
Matted hair and weird earrings I'll
dress up as Śiva
and bring the dead yogin to life.
Dark One, it's your fault that Surdās
has only one theme—
the torment of a god's disappearance.
Body and mind
burnt to cinder, it's ash he
offers
his Dark One.

:AS

Black night without love
is a she-cobra.
If the moon would rise I could
turn back the sting.
But spells have proved futile
charms worthless—
now even love is extinguished.
Without his Dark Lord, Sur is a lost
snakebitten girl
convulsing with
venom.

:AS

Surdās

SURDĀS IS THE renowned blind bhakti poet of North India. Along with Mirabai, he remains one of the most commonly presented by classical singers on the concert hall stage. An enormous corpus of songs attributed to him—amounting to four or five thousand but legendarily numbered at one hundred thousand *padas*—are collectively titled the *Sursagar*, the "Ocean of Sur." (*Pada* is the loose term used all over Northern India for a poem or song-lyric. It stems from the Sanskrit, and literally means "foot," referring to metrical feet.) Reliable facts about Surdās's life have been long veiled by a sectarian hagiography, recorded in the *Cauri Vaisnavan ki Varta,* or "Conversation with Eighty-four Vaishnavas," attributed to Gokulnath, whose birthdate of 1551 suggests that as a young man he might conceivably have met an elderly Surdās.

As with Mirabai, whose life also overlaps Surdās's, what survives in written record and in popular culture cannot all be the work of a single author. We would do better to refer to a Surdās tradition, added on to by dozens or even hundreds of singers from the sixteenth century until recent times. The name, or more properly, the title, Surdās, has come to be used as a respectful address to a blind man, especially blind singers, met all over India today.

⦂ Dadu Dayal
(1544—1604)

Sākhīs

I tell the truth,
there's no doubt about it—
whoever takes the life of another creature
goes the dark
road to hell.

. . . .

They cut animal throats, says Dadu—
and claim it's their faith.
Five times a day at their prayers
standing on nothing.

. . . .

The Lord of Wisdom, says Dadu
throws dice.
Nobody watches him.
He rules the universe and
you can't stain him.

There's a worm called Time
drilling into your body.
Every day, says Dadu, the end
draws closer.

. . . .

He wouldn't hurt his relatives
but heretics he'd kill.
Dadu says: you won't see the light
if you don't
kill yourself.

. . . .

The worn-out clay pitcher is broken
that once had nine holes.
Did you imagine, asks Dadu,
it held water forever?

AS

Dadu Dayal

B ORN IN AHMEDABAD to low-caste parents, Dadu was a Tom of Bedlam or Crazy Jane truth-speaker. His life is closely associated with various districts in Gujarat and Rajasthan, and he may have lived in a cave beneath the "amber fort" of Amer for some time. Some say his father found him as a child adrift in a river, his cradle swirling downstream, and brought him home. Probably this is a later story intended to provide him a proper Brahman birth, and to erase the painful low-caste status so his poetry would seem properly orthodox.

Called Dayal, "the compassionate," Dadu by caste and upbringing was a cotton-carder—an occupation in which low-status Hindus live at close quarters with Muslims. He drew the wrath of both religions for publicly spurning their scriptures. Ritual he savagely mocked— especially animal sacrifice, which he considered repulsive. His *sākhīs* (literally "witness" poems, two lines in the original Braj Bhaṣa dialect) owe much to Kabir and other North Indian poet-saints. A sect founded in his name, the Dadu Panth (creed or "path" of Dadu), exists to this day in Rajasthan. Painted images the Panth has produced show a youthful, turbaned, holy man. He wears a white robe, sports a thin moustache, and emanates tranquility, while a halo of golden light surrounds his head. I find this sanctified image hard to square with Dadu's razor-toothed *sākhīs*, full of warnings about inevitable death, and blistering at hollow displays of holiness.

⦂ Panjabi Songs

(SUNG BY USTĀD ABDUL RAHĪM; RECORDED AND
TRANSLATED BY ANANDA COOMARASWAMY, CIRCA 1913)

I

When I go down to draw water, O Mother, at Jamna ghat
He catches my clothes and twists my hand—
When I go to sell milk,
At every step Gokula seeks to stop me.
He is so obstinate, what can I say?
He ever comes and goes: why does this Youngling so?
He seizes my arm and shuts my mouth and holds me close:
I will make my complaint to Kans Raja, then I shall have no fear
of Thee!

II

See, Sakhis, how Krishna stands!
How can I go fetch water, my mother-in-law?
When I go to draw water from Jamna,
There meets me the young boy of Nand!

III

What yogi is this, with rings in his ears and ashes smeared, who
wanders about?
Some perform meditation, some dwell in the woods, some call on
Thy name with devotion!

IV

To the hem of thy garment I cling, O Rama!
My refuge Thou art:
Thou art my Lord—
To the hem of thy garment I cling, O Rama!

V

How can I loosen the knot that binds the heart of my beloved?
All my comrades well-decked are embraced by their lovers,
But I sit alone eating poison.

VI

My Lord has not spoken, he sulks since the afternoon—
The wheat crops are ripe, the rose trees in bloom.
I need not thy earnings, only come to the Panjāb again!
Thou farest away on thy journey, but I am left desolate:
Oh! the empty house and the courtyard fill me with fear—
The wheat crops are ripe, the rose trees in bloom.

:AC

Panjabi Songs

Art historian Ananda Coomaraswamy and his wife, the British singer Ratan Devī, collected these lyrics and published them in 1913. Translated by Coomaraswamy, these versions—resting on the cusp between devotion and love song—are examples of the type of neo-Victorian translation that has largely disappeared from the English-speaking world. Within a year or two of their publication, modernism—Ezra Pound in particular—would sweep from England the grammatical inversions ("there meets me the young boy"), the capitalized *Thee* and *Thou*, and other archaisms. But Coomaraswamy's translations are classics of their sort. He also gives an account of the singer, Ustād Abdul Rahīm, from whom he received the songs in their original Panjabi:

> His ancestors were Brāhmans, forcibly converted at the time of Aurangzeb. Like many other Panjābī Musulmāns in the same case, the family retain many Hindu customs, e.g., non-remarriage of widows. Abdul Rahīm's faith in Hindu gods is as strong as his belief in Islām and Moslem saints, and he sings with equal earnestness of Krishna or Allah, exemplifying the complete fusion of Hindu and Moslem tradition characteristic of so many parts of northern India today. He is devout and even superstitious; he would hesitate to sing *dīpak rāg*, unless in very cold weather.

Dīpak is the raga of the "lamp," associated with fire. Musicians consider it dangerous and only the most adept would attempt it. Tansen, who invented it, a renowned musician at the court of Emperor Akbar, is said to have sung it reluctantly—the palace lamps began to flare dangerously—but disaster was averted because he'd instructed his wife to sing a rain raga in a nearby location at the same time.

These Panjabi lyrics refer to Krishna, Rama, and Śiva; a few may simply be love songs.

: JAYADEVA

A VERSE CYCLE FROM THE *GĪTA-GOVINDA*
(TWELFTH CENTURY)

"Clouds thicken the sky,
the forests are
dark with tamala trees.
He is afraid of night, Radha,
take him home."
They depart at Nanda's directive
passing on the way
thickets of trees.
But reaching Yamuna River, secret desires
overtake Radha and Krishna.

Jayadeva, chief poet on pilgrimage
to Padmavati's feet—
every craft of
Goddess Language
stored in his heart—
has assembled tales from the erotic encounters
of Krishna and Śrī
to compose these cantos.

If thoughts of Krishna
    make your heart moody;
if arts of courtship
    stir something deep;
Then listen to Jayadeva's songs
    flooded with tender music.

Krishna stirs every
creature on earth.
Archaic longing awakens.
He initiates Love's
holy rite with languorous blue
lotus limbs.
Cowherd girls like
splendid wild animals draw him into their
bodies for pleasure—
It is spring. Krishna at play
is eros incarnate.

Krishna roamed the forest
taking the cowherdesses one after
another for love.
Radha's hold slackened,
jealousy drove her far off.
But over each refuge
in the vine-draped thickets
swarmed a loud circle of bees.
Miserable
she confided the secret
to her friend—

Radha speaks

My conflicted heart
treasures even his infidelities.
Won't admit anger.
Forgives the deceptions.
Secret desires rise in my breasts.
What can I do? Krishna
hungry for lovers
slips off without me.
This torn heart grows only
more ardent.

His hand loosens from the
bamboo flute.
A tangle of pretty
eyes draws him down.
Moist excitement on his cheeks.
Krishna catches me
eyeing him in a grove
swarmed by young women—
I stare at his smiling baffled face
and get aroused.

Krishna speaks

Every touch brought a new thrill.
Her eyes darted wildly.
From her mouth the
fragrance of lotus,
a rush of sweet forbidden words.
A droplet of juice
on her crimson lower lip.
My mind fixes these absent
sensations in a *samādhi*—
How is it that parted from her
the oldest
wound breaks open?

Radha's messenger speaks

Her house has become
a pulsating jungle.
Her circle of girlfriends
a tightening snare.
Each time she breathes
a sheet of flame
bursts above the trees.
Krishna, you have gone—
in your absence she takes shape
as a doe crying out—
while Love turns to Death
and closes in
on tiger paws.

Sick with feverish
urges.
Only the poultice of your body
can heal her, holy physician of the heart.
Free her from torment, Krishna—
or are you
cruel as a thunderbolt?

The messenger speaks to Radha

Krishna lingers
in the thicket
where together you mastered the secrets
of lovemaking.
Fixed in meditation,
sleepless
he chants a sequence of mantras.
He has one burning desire—
to draw *amṛta*
from your offered breasts.

Sighs, short repeated gasps—
he glances around helpless.
The thicket deserted.
He pushes back in, his breath
comes in a rasp.
He rebuilds the couch of blue floral branches.
Steps back and studies it.
Radha, precious Radha!
Your lover turns on a wheel,
image after
feverish image.

She ornaments her limbs
if a single leaf stirs
in the forest.
She thinks it's you, folds back
the bedclothes and stares
in rapture for hours.
Her heart conceives a hundred
amorous games on the well-prepared bed.
But without you this
wisp of a girl
will fade
to nothing tonight.

At nightfall
the crater-pocked moon as though
exposing a crime
slips onto the paths of
girls who seek lovers.
It casts a platinum web
over Vrindavan forest's dark hollows—
a sandalwood spot
on the proud face of sky.

The brindled moon soars above.
Krishna waits underneath.
And Radha
wrenched with grief
is alone.

The lonely moon
pale as Krishna's sad, far-off
lotus-face has
calmed my thoughts.
O but the moon is also Love's planet—
a wild desolation
strikes through my heart.

Let the old doubts go,
anguished Radha.
Your unfathomed breasts and
cavernous loins
are all I desire.
What other girl has the power?
Love is a ghost
that has slipped into my entrails.
When I reach to embrace your
deep breasts
may we fulfill the rite
we were born for—

Krishna for hours
entreated
the doe-eyed girl
then returned to his thicket bed and dressed.
Night fell again.
Radha, unseen, put on radiant gems.
A girlish voice pressed her—
go swiftly.

Her companion reports—

"She'll look into me—
tell love tales—
chafing with pleasure she'll draw me—
into her body—
drakṣyati vakṣyati ramsyate"
   —he's fearful,
   he glances about. He shivers for you,
bristles, calls wildly, sweats, goes forward,
reels back.
The dark thicket closes
about him

Eyes dark with kohl
ears bright with creamy tamala petals
a black lotus headdress and breasts
traced with musk-leaf—
In every thicket, friend,
Night's precious cloak wraps a girl's limbs.
The veiled affairs
the racing heart—

Eager, fearful, ecstatic—
darting her eyes across Govinda she
enters the thicket.
    Ankles ringing with silver.

Her friends have slipped off.
Her lower lip's moist
wistful, chaste, swollen, trembling, deep.
He sees her raw heart
sees her eyes rest on the couch of
fresh flowering twigs
and speaks.

Sung to Rāga Vibhāsa

Come, Radha, come. Krishna follows your
every desire.

"Soil my bed with indigo footprints, *Kaminī,*
lay waste the grove
savage it with your petal-soft feet.

"I take your feet in lotus hands, *Kaminī,*
you have come far.
Lay these gold flaring anklets across my bed.

"Let *yes yes* flow from your mouth like *amṛta.*
From your breasts, *Kaminī,*
I draw off the *dukūla*-cloth. We are no longer separate."

Sung to Rāga Rāmakari

She sings while Krishna plays, her heart drawn
into ecstasy—

"On my breast, your hand Krishna
cool as sandalwood. Draw a leaf wet with deer musk here,
it is Love's sacramental jar.

"Drape my loins with jeweled belts, fabric and gemstones.
My *mons venus* is brimming with nectar,
a cave mouth for thrusts of Desire."

Reckless, inflamed, she presses forth
to the urgent campaign
of sexual love,
flips over and mounts him,
savors the way
he gives in . . .

. . . later, eyes lidded,
loins cool and no longer rippling,
her arms trail like vines.
Only her chest continues to heave.
Is climbing on top
    what brought her victory?

Reader, open your heart
to Jayadeva's well-
crafted poem. Through it
Krishna's deeds have entered your own memory-stream—
amṛta to cure
    Kali Yuga's contagion.

Coda

On my breast draw a leaf
paint my cheeks
lay a silk scarf across these dark loins.
Wind into my heavy black braid
white petals,
fit gemstones onto my wrists,
anklets over my feet.

Each affection she asked for
her saffron robed lover
fulfilled.

:AS

Jayadeva

THE TWELFTH-CENTURY *GĪTA-GOVINDA* of Jayadeva has a reputation as the last great poem in the Sanskrit language. It holds two other distinctions. First, it appears to be the first full account in poetry of Radha as Krishna's favorite among the *gopi*s or cowgirls of Vrindavana. Secondly, it seems to be the first historical instance of poetry written with specified ragas or musical modes assigned to its lyrics. The poem-cycle occurs in twelve cantos with twenty-four songs distributed among them, about 280 stanzas in total. It presents the love affair of Krishna and Radha as an acutely human love affair, from initial "secret desires" and urgent lovemaking to separation—nights of betrayal, mistrust, longing, feverish anguish, strange imaginings—and finally to a consummation as spiritual as it is carnal.

Jayadeva's birthplace is uncertain—some think Orissa, some Mithila, some Bengal. Accounts make it clear he had carefully trained himself as a poet in the Sanskrit tradition, learnéd and in command of classical metrics, when he took a vow to wander as a homeless mendicant, to sleep no more than one night under any tree. On this endless pilgrimage he passed through the coastal city of Puri in Orissa State, one of India's cardinal pilgrim destinations and home to the huge Jagannath Temple. There in Puri, the chief priest and administrator of the Jagannath Temple had a vision. In it Krishna told him that Jayadeva should marry his daughter Padmāvatī, a dancer dedicated to the temple, settle down, and compose a devotional poem of unprecedented beauty to Krishna. The result was the *Gīta-govinda*.

At one point while composing his poem, overwhelmed that he had to write words that belonged to Krishna, Jayadeva, unable to continue, put down his stylus and went to the river to bathe. When he returned he asked for his meal. Padmāvatī exclaimed that she had already fed him. Confused, Jayadeva looked at his manuscript; the words he had felt unable to compose sat inked onto the palm-leaf page. Krishna had visited in Jayadeva's absence and taken a hand in his own poem—then, mischievously disguised as the poet, stayed on to eat Jayadeva's lunch.

Meeting Padmāvatī wakened in Jayadeva the bedrock emotion, the *rasa*, of love. What had been distant accounts of spiritual grace, a familiar theme for poetry, or even a set of metaphysical abstractions, came alive in his own body: the merging of spiritual and erotic ecstasy. Under Padmāvatī's hands Jayadeva learnt that the old tales, the yogic teachings, and the cycles of loss and longing were no far-off vision. They are tasted through one's senses.

You could say that all the metaphysics and yoga practices of India—heady, magnificent, intricate, contradictory—return in the end to a single imperative: love. I think it the genius of Radha-Krishna poetry to take the hair-splitting metaphysics of India, lift them from our easily bewildered minds, and relocate them in the glands of the human body. Krishna devotees say that in our current dark era, the Kali Yuga, not everyone can practice meditation; few can wrap their minds around subtle doctrine or follow the eight stages of yoga. Everyone can taste the desolations and ecstasies of love, though; this is where one finds Krishna.

Some centuries after Jayadeva's death, the Jagannatha Temple instituted the *Gīta-govinda* as its sole liturgy, with Padmāvatī's dances performed in the sanctuary. All day and into the evening loudspeakers mounted on poles around the temple send the poem in loud song across courtyard and rooftop, out to the cashew groves and semi-arid scrublands threaded by jackal and cobras.

: Vidyāpati

(1352—1448?)

The girl and the woman
bound in one being:
the girl puts up her hair,
the woman lets it
fall to cover her breasts;
the girl reveals her arms,
her long legs, innocently bold;
the woman wraps her shawl modestly about her,
her open glance a little veiled.
Restless feet, a blush on the young breasts,
hint at her heart's disquiet:
behind her closed eyes
Kāma awakes, born in imagination, the god.

Vidyāpati says, O Krishna, bridegroom,
be patient, she will be brought to you.

:DL & ECD

My friend, I cannot answer when you ask me to
        explain
what has befallen me.
Love is transformed, renewed,
each moment.
He has dwelt in my eyes all the days of my life,
yet I am not sated with seeing.
My ears have heard his sweet voice in eternity,
and yet it is always new to them.
How many honeyed nights have I passed with him
in love's bliss, yet my body
wonders at his.
Through all the ages
he has been clasped to my breast,
yet my desire
never abates.
I have seen subtle people sunk in passion
but none came so close to the heart of the fire.

Who shall be found to cool your heart,
says Vidyāpati.

:DL & ECD

With the last of my garments
shame dropped from me, fluttered
to earth and lay discarded at my feet.
My lover's body became
the only covering I needed.
With bent head he gazed at the lamp
like a bee who desires the honey of a closed lotus.
The Mind-stealing One, like the *chātaka* bird,
is wanton, he misses no chance
to gratify his thirst; I was to him
a pool of raindrops.
                    Now shame returns
as I remember. My heart trembles,
recalling his treachery.

So Vidyāpati says.

:DL & ECD

May none other be born to this world. But if it must
     be,
let it not be a girl that is born.
But if a girl must be born, let her not know
the agony that is called 'love.'
But if she must know it, let her not be
a girl of gentle breeding.
Wretched women pray for one thing: God,
let me know peace at last. Let me unite
with a husband wise and skilled, a fountain of love,
and let his love not fall into the power of another.
But if it does, may he be considerate,
for a woman is not wholly lost if she is treated with
     kindness.

Vidyāpati says: There is a way.
By your own life you can gain the far shore of this
     sea of conflict.

                                        :DL & ECD

I who body and soul
am at your beck and call,
was a girl of noble family.
I took no thought of what would be said of me,
I abandoned everything:
now I am part of you,
your will is my will.
O Mādhava, never let our love
seem to grow stale—
I beg you, let the dew
not dry on our flowers,
that my honor not be destroyed.

When he heard these words from her beautiful
        mouth, Mādhava
bowed his head. He knew he held
the flower of her life in his keeping.

:DL & ECD

Her friend speaks:

Her cloud of hair eclipses the luster of her face,
    like Rāhu greedy for the moon;
the garland glitters in her unbound hair, a wave of
    the Ganges in the waters of the Yamunā.
How beautiful the deliberate, sensuous union of the
    two; the girl playing this time the active role,
riding her lover's outstretched body in delight;
her smiling lips shine with drops of sweat; the god
    of love offering pearls to the moon.
She of beautiful face hotly kisses the mouth of her
    beloved; the moon, with face bent down,
    drinks of the lotus.
The garland hanging on her heavy breast seems like
    a stream of milk from golden jars.
The tinkling bells which decorate her hips sound the
    triumphal music of the god of love.

:DL & ECD

O my friend, my sorrow is unending.
It is the rainy season, my house is empty,
the sky is filled with seething clouds,
the earth sodden with rain,
and my love far away.

Cruel Kāma pierces me with his arrows:
the lightning flashes, the peacocks dance,
frogs and waterbirds, drunk with delight,
call incessantly—and my heart is heavy.
Darkness on earth,
the sky intermittently lit with a sullen glare . . .

Vidyāpati says,
How will you pass this night without your lord?

:DL & ECD

When my beloved returns to my house
I shall make my body a temple of gladness,
I shall make my body the altar of joy
and let down my hair to sweep it.
My twisting necklace of pearls shall be the intricate
sprinkled design on the altar,
my full breasts the water jars,
my curved hips the plantain trees,
the tinkling bells at my waist the young shoots of the
     mango.
I shall use the arcane arts of fair women in all lands
to make my beauty outshine a thousand moons.

Soon your hopes, O Rādhā, says Vidyāpati,
will be fulfilled, and he will be at your side.

:DL & ECD

The moon has shone upon me,
the face of my beloved.
O night of joy!

Joy permeates all things.
My life: joy,
my youth: fulfillment.

Today my house is again
home,
   today my body is
my body.
   The god
of destiny smiled on me.
No more doubt.

Let the nightingales sing, then,
let there be myriad
rising moons, let Kāma's
five arrows become five thousand
and the south wind

softly, softly blow:
for now my body has meaning
in the presence of my beloved.

Vidyāpati says, Your luck is great;
may this return of love be blessed.

:DL & ECD

Children, wife, friend—
drops of water on heated sand.
I spent myself on them, forgetting you.
What are they to me now,
O Mādhava, now that I am old and without hope,
apart from you. But you are the savior of the world
and full of mercy.
       Half my life I passed in sleep—
my youth, now my old age,
how much time.
I spent my youth in lust and dissipation.
I had no time to worship you.
       Ageless gods
have come and passed away.
Born from you, they enter you again
like waves into the sea.
For you have no beginning, and no end.
             Now
at the end, I fear
the messengers of Death.
Apart from you, there is no way.
I call you Lord,
the infinite and finite,
my salvation.

:DL & ECD

Vidyāpati

VIDYĀPATI WROTE two hundred years after Jayadeva composed his *Gīta-govinda*, picking up Jayadeva's theme. However, the story cycle was well-known by the late fourteenth century, and rather than retelling the story or outlining a dramatic cycle in verse, he devised songs in his own language, Maithili, that could be situated within the story. Following the convention of devotional poetry, he inserted himself by name at the close of each poem, stepping in to address the lovers, now and then with a light mocking humor. This "signature line" is called a *bhānita*.

Vidyāpati was a court poet in the region of Mithila, trained in the twin arts of poetry and erotic love. His solitary theme—with the exception of a few heartbroken songs like "Children, wife, friend," above—was the eros of Krishna and Radha. Given the acute passion of his poems, it is reasonable to think he regarded the lovemaking of the dark god and his favorite *gopi*, or cowherding girl, not as metaphor, but as the self's actual union with god.

For the first portion of his adult life Vidyāpati served as the favorite poet and confidant of the warlord Śivasimha. It is possible the poet was celebrating his patron in these songs, praising Śivasimha's virility and charm, and the poems are thinly disguised panegyrics or praise poems to a king. Whatever his motive for writing them, Vidyāpati must have seen sexual love as the deepest need and profoundest experience a human can undergo. Simply to experience longing, heartwrenching desire, sexual rapture, stabs of jealousy, or romantic anguish, draws one into the sphere of Krishna. Theology of his day would have affirmed this. In his poems even anguish, grief, or hopeless ardent passion become pure emotions—*rasa*s—transporting the lovers into Krishna's presence. Śivasimha assigned a singer named Jayata to set each of Vidyāpati's poems to a particular raga or musical mode. The lyrics went to dancing girls at the court who choreographed them. As song and dance they spread across Mithila and into the adjacent districts of Bengal.

Vidyāpati composed his Krishna-Radha poems from about 1380 until 1406, the year his patron Śivasimha vanished after a military defeat at Muslim hands. At that point he took up composing dry philosophical works in Sanskrit, and seems never to have revisited poems of the *prem bhakti marg*, the path of love and devotion. He lived forty years beyond his patron's presumed death, composing work that seems comparatively joyless. When exactly he died is uncertain.

My mind is not on housework.
Now I weep, now I laugh at the world's
censure.
   He draws me—to become
an outcast, a hermit woman in the woods!
He has bereft me of parents, brothers, sisters,
my good name. His flute
took my heart—
his flute, a thin bamboo trap enclosing me—
a cheap bamboo flute was Rādhā's ruin.
That hollow, simple stick—
fed nectar by his lips, but issuing
poison . . .

If you should find
a clump of jointed reeds,
pull off their branches!
Tear them up by the roots!
Throw them
    into the sea.

Dvija Chandidāsa says, Why the bamboo?
Not it but Krishna enthralls you: him you cannot
   uproot.

:DL & ECD

This dark cloudy night
he'll not come to me . . .
But yes, he is here!
He stands dripping with rain
in the courtyard. O my heart!

What virtue accrued in
another life has brought me
such bliss? I who
fear my elders and dare not go out to him?
I who torment him? I see

his sorrow and deep love
and I am tormented.
I would set fire to my house
for him, I would bear
the scorn of the world.

He thinks his sorrow is joy,
when I weep he weeps.

When it comes to know such depth of love
the heart of the world will rejoice,
says Chandidāsa.

:DL & ECD

I brought honey and drank it mixed with milk—
but where was its sweetness? I tasted gall.
I am steeped in bitterness, as the seed
of a bitter fruit in its juice.
My heart smolders.
A fire without is plain to be seen
but this fire flames within,
it sears my breast.
Desire burns the body—how can it be relieved?

By the touch of Kānu, says Chandidāsa.

:DL & ECD

Love, what can I say to you?
I was too young to love,
but you did not let me stay at home.
I shall drown myself in the sea
with this last wish:
That I be born again as Nanda's son
and you as Rādhā.
Then, after loving you, I shall abandon you.
I shall stand beneath the *kadamba* tree;
I shall stand in the *tribhanga* pose and play my flute
as you go to draw water.
And when you hear the flute you will be enchanted,
simple girl.

Chandidāsa says, Then you will know
how love can burn.

:DL & ECD

Suddenly I am afraid.
At any moment, Kānu's love for me may cease.
A building can collapse because of a single flaw—
who knows in what ways I, who desire to be
a palace for his pleasure, may be faulty?
And few are those who can restore
what once is broken . . .
Distracted, I wander
from place to place, everywhere finding
only anxiety. Oh, to see
his smile!
    My love,
whoever brings down the house of our love
will have murdered a woman!

Chandidāsa says, O Rādhā, you reflect too much;
without your love he could not live a moment.

:DL & ECD

My faults, my jealousy, are
woman's nature—
O my heart, Kānāi,
do not be angry.
Did not you, yourself,
use the same words—
'Do not be angry'?—
and now all my anger is gone.
See, awakening at your feet,
my heart, Kānāi. Ah,
do not think of others as you do of me,
the god of love has woven in a garland
your heart and mine,
and I will do as you desire, in Vrindāvana.
Has not God made one body and one soul
of your love and mine? Then it is not my doing
if you must not take your love to another,
but the will of God . . .
One by one I turn your virtues over in my mind—
come, sit beside me,

sings Badu Chandidāsa.

:DL & ECD

Beloved, what more shall I say to you?
In life and in death, in birth after birth
you are the lord of my life.
A noose of love binds
my heart to your feet.
My mind fixed on you alone, I have offered you
          everything;
in truth, I have become your slave.
In this family, in that house, who is really mine?
Whom can I call my own?
It was bitter cold, and I took refuge
at your lotus feet.
While my eyes blink, and I do not see you,
I feel the heart within me die.

A touchstone
I have threaded and wear upon my throat,
says Chandidāsa.

:DL & ECD

Chandidāsa

FOR SIX CENTURIES songs have circulated in Bengal with the name Chandidāsa attached. When scholars winnow through and isolate poems they can trace authentically to a historical figure of the fifteenth century, they still find four figures using variants of the name: Chandidāsa, Dwija Chandidās, Badu Chandidāsa, and Dina Chandidāsa. Nobody can say whether these were four separate poets or only one. Scholars—using theological principles in the songs—propose two Chandidāsas, a later one belonging to a deviant sect called the *sahajiyā*. The Chandidāsa story that circulates with the songs portrays a single poet, known as the chief *rasika bhakta*, or devotee of love—pure, untarnished love. Unlike other bhakti poets of the period—Vidyāpati a ready example—Chandidāsa seems little touched by the influence of Sanskrit poetry. Almost all of it speaks in the voice of Radha or Krishna, spurred by a passion that stems from his own life.

Chandidāsa—the original one—likely came from Nanur, a village in the Birbhum region of Bengal. A Brahman dedicated to the temple of the local goddess Bashuli, Chandidāsa fell in love with a young woman named Rāmī who had appeared at the temple looking for work. Rāmī was a low-caste washerwoman who took to scrubbing the temple courtyard. She was supposed to remain invisible to the priests and high-caste worshippers. Her affair with Chandidāsa scandalized the village. The lovers were reviled and may have been expelled from the community.

To complicate Chandidāsa's story—who he was or who wrote the poems attributed to him—many of his poems are in Radha's voice. This was a convention that poets in India had practiced for centuries. About two hundred years ago, though, a manuscript surfaced, a "sheaf of poems," containing verse composed after Chandidāsa's death. Based on their contents, scholars attribute the poems to Rāmī, or Rāmonī, the beloved for whose sake Chandidāsa wrote:

> I throw ashes at all laws
> Made by man or god.
> What is the worth
> Of your vile laws
> That failed me
> In love?
> (DB translation)

Rāmī figures intimately into Chandidāsa's death. The *nawab* of Gaur had invited Chandidāsa to sing at his court, and his queen, the *begum*, went into rapture at the poet's performance. An electric passion passed from the *begum* to Chandidāsa, the intensity of her sexual desire visible to all who were present. The *nawab* flew into a fury. He had Chandidāsa roped across the spine of an elephant and ordered the palace guards to flog him to death.

The *nawab* forced his wife to watch the public torture and execution. Rāmī too watched on in horror, Chandidāsa all the time fixing his gaze on her—the person for whom he'd lived—until he lost consciousness. The *begum* was devastated, and shortly afterwards killed herself. What became of Rāmī, nobody knows, but her manuscript of poems that came to light centuries later are full of rage at hierarchy and political oppression.

One poem of Chandidāsa's begins, in Deben Bhattacharya's translation,

> The essence of beauty
> springs from the eternal play
> of man as Krishna

and woman as Radha.
Devoted lovers
in the act of loving, seek to reach
the goal...

It closes with an assertion that sounds acutely modern—a phrase
that became a touchstone for poets of the Bengali Renaissance and
through the twentieth century. Whether by "man" Chandidāsa
means Humanity or the mystical inward Self, who can tell?

Listen, O brother man,
Man is the greatest Truth
Of all,
Nothing beyond.
(DB translation)

⁝ GOVINDA-DĀSA
(1535—1613)

When they had made love
she lay in his arms in the *kunja* grove.
Suddenly she called his name
and wept—as if she burned in the fire of
separation.
>   The gold was in her *anchal*
>   but she looked afar for it!
—Where has he gone? Where has my love gone?
O why has he left me alone?
And she writhed on the ground in despair,
only her pain kept her from fainting.
Krishna was astonished
and could not speak.

Taking her beloved friend by the hand,
Govinda-dāsa led her softly away.

⁝DL & ECD

When you listened to the sound
of Krishna's flute,
I stopped your ears.
When you gazed at the beauty
of his body,
I covered your eyes.
You were angry.
O lovely one, I told you then
that if you let love grow in you
your life would pass in tears.
You offered him your body,
you wanted his touch—
you did not ask if he would be kind.
And now each day your beauty
fades a little more;
how much longer can you live?
You planted in your heart
the tree of love,
in hope of nourishment
from that dark cloud.
Now water it
with your tears,

says Govinda-dāsa.

:DL & ECD

Govinda-dāsa

ORN IN BENGAL a century after Vidyāpati's final years, Govin-
da-dāsa is said to have begun life as a Śakta, or goddess-worship-
per, before dedicating himself to the enormous spiritual revival of
the sixteenth century that focused on Krishna and Radha. He loved
Vidyāpati's poetry, and traveled to the earlier poet's home village,
Bishpi, in order to collect all he could.

Rabindranath Tagore set one of Govinda-dāsa's poems to music,
and Krishna-Radha devotees still sing them today.

The poem "When they had made love" plays on the notion that
humans long for the divine and will search faraway places, when in
fact the spirit is with us all the time. An *anchal* is the corner of the sari
that Indian women wear over the shoulder; in Bengal they use it as a
purse, tying into it money, personal items, or jewelry.

⦂ Rāmprasād Sen

(CIRCA 1718—1775)

I spent my days in fun,
Now, Time's up and I'm out of a job.
I used to go here and there making money,
Had brothers, friends, wife, and children
Who listened when I spoke. Now they scream at me
Just because I'm poor. Death's
Field man is going to sit by my pillow
Waiting to grab my hair, and my friends
And relations will stack up the bier,
Fill the pitcher, ready my shroud and say
So long to the old boy
In his holy man's get-up.
They'll shout Hari a few times,
Dump me on the pile and walk off.
That's it for old Rāmprasād.
They'll wipe off the tears
And dig in for their supper.

⦂LN & CS

Listen to this story, Mother Tara,
My house is a battlefield, nothing but a quarrel
Of cross purposes, Five Senses,
Mother, each with a different desire,
All wanting pleasure all the time.

I have been born in eight million forms
And now I'm born a man,
A funny figure in a world
Whose gift to us is a load of misery.

Mother, look at Rāmprasād
Trying to live in this house
Whose master is driven crazy,
Beaten by the Six Tenants.

:LN & CS

How many times, Mother, are you going
To trundle me on this wheel like a blind-
Folded ox grinding out oil? You've got me
Tied to this old trunk of a world, flogging me
On and on. What have I done to be forced to serve
These Six Oily Dealers, the Passions?
All these births—eighty times 100,000—
As beast and bird and still the door
Of the womb is not shut on me
And I come out hurting once more!
When a child cries out, calling the precious name
Of mother, then a mother takes it in her arms.
Everywhere I look I see that's the rule,
Except for me. All some sinners need to do
Is shout "Durgā" and—pouf!—they're saved.

Take this blindfold off so I can see
The feet that give comfort. There are many
Bad children, but who ever heard
Of a bad mother?

There's only one hope
For Rāmprasād, Mother—that in the end
He will be safe at Your feet.

:LN & CS

Does suffering scare me? O Mother,
Let me suffer in this world. Do I require more?
Suffering runs ahead of me and runs after me.
I carry it on my head and set up a stand
In a bazaar to peddle it.
I'm a poison worm, I thrive on poison.
I carry it wherever I go.

Prasād says: Mother, lift off my load.
I need a little rest. It's amazing!
Others brag about their happiness,
I brag about my suffering.

LN & CS

You'll find Mother
In any house.

Do I dare say it in public?

She is Bhairavī with Shiva,
Durgā with Her children,
Sītā with Lakshmaṇa.

She's mother, daughter, wife, sister—
Every woman close to you.

What more can Rāmprasād say?
You work the rest out from these hints.

:LN & CS

That's it, Mother!
The play is done.
It's over, my Happy One.
I came into this world
To play, took the dust
Of this world and played,
And now, Daughter of High Places,
Suddenly I'm scared. Death is so near,
So serious. I think of those games
I played as a boy, and all that breath
Wasted in the pleasure of marriage
When it should have gone for prayer.

Rāmprasād begs: Mother,
Old age has broken me—what do I do now?
Mother, teach this worshipper
Worship, plunge me
Into the saving waves.

:LN & CS

[After Rāmprasād Sen]

Arms shielding my face
Knees drawn up
Falling through flicker
Of womb after womb,
    through worlds,
Only begging, Mother,
      must I be born again?

Snyder says: you bear me, nurse me
I meet you, always love you,
    you dance
   on my chest and thigh

Forever born again.

:GS

Rāmprasād Sen

THE KNOWN FACTS of Rāmprasād's life would fit into a matchbox. He was born in the Bengali village of Halisahar somewhere between 1718 and 1723. He may have served for a time as a clerk in a Calcutta merchant house, where he is said to have filled up his account ledgers with hymns to Kali. After leaving the regular workforce, he returned to Halisahar; his early biographer, Iśvarcandra Gupta, records him receiving a land grant in 1758 from the maharaja who would become his patron, Krsnacandra Ray.

Rāmprasād's death dates vary between 1762 and 1803, a confounding range of forty-one years. An oil portrait exists, reportedly of the poet, by English painter Arthur William Devis, painted in the early 1790s. Though Rāmprasād would have been in his early seventies, the portrait shows a youngish man clad in a twisted loincloth, dreadlocks longer than his body; he leans relaxedly against a banyan tree; a rubbed votive stone depicting Vishnu and his two wives tilts among the tree's massive roots.

Two stories about Rāmprasād stand out. The first recounts how his Calcutta employer, discovering Rāmprasād scrawling hymns to Kali in the margins of the account books, found either the poems so good or the poet's devotion so convincing that he sent the poet home with a stipend to continue composing. The other tells how Rāmprasād vanished—as many bhakti poets did—in a self-willed act of devotion. At Kali Puja, on the day of the goddess's immersion in the river near Halisahar, Rāmprasād carried the *mūrti* or image of Kali on his head into the waters. He submerged himself along with the goddess, and as he sank below the surface his *brahmarandra*—the aperture at the top of the skull where the spirit escapes—split open. He died singing the lines of his final poem.

Gary Snyder's poem "[After Rāmprasād Sen]" cannot exactly be called a translation. However, it draws directly from extant songs. Its stripped-down wording and distribution of phrases on the page edge closer to Rāmprasād's syntax than versions which may follow a Bengali verse with literal correctness, but lack the use of breath and spacing that make you feel like you're falling through "flicker / Of womb after womb."

In our day it is impossible to tell which poems a historical Rāmprasād wrote, and which were composed by other poets or singers and passed on with Rāmprasād's name in their signature lines. If you think of "Rāmprasād Sen" as a vision-through-song-lineage of the past two and a half centuries, then Snyder's poem stands right in that bloodline. It is as close to its model as Robert Bly's Kabir versions are to any flesh-and-blood Kabir. The one difference: Snyder inserts his own name in the signature line, not Rāmprasād's as Bengali street singers have done for two and a half centuries.

A glimpse of how hard it is to pin down an actual Rāmprasād comes from an account by Iśvarcandra Gupta, who went in search of poems in about 1853, fifty to ninety years after the poet's death.

> Works of his which had been collected earlier have by now almost disappeared, because in those days people used to guard them carefully like some secret mantra, not showing them to anyone even at the cost of their lives, bringing them out at puja time to decorate with flowers and sandalwood paste, as some people still do today, and though we would have given all we had we were not able to obtain any of the verses. Hidden in this way they have become completely destroyed. Worms and other insects ate them, moisture decomposed them, fire burned them, they were

used by the impotent as charms to secure beautiful women or long life. . . .

In this atmosphere legends have curled like smoke through cracks in the courtyard tiles. Poems with a signature line of Rāmprasād Sen continue to show up in Bengal. Their tone doesn't waver much: petition, complaint, truculent demand, distress, fitful temper tantrum, frustration, childish fury. A long history of *ninda-stuti*, "praise in the form of abusive reproach," exists in India, but there are few poems like Rāmprasād's. His steam with childish fits, thrown to catch the attention of a mother he rebukes for ignoring him—a mother who frequents cremation grounds with her ganja-smoking minions, who dances among jackals and crows, leaving her child unprotected, whimpering, and unfed.

Here, where the secrets of childhood twist in helpless discomfort, is where Kali the dark goddess, stark and unapproachable, appears. Laden with Tantric ciphers and primitive symbols, Rāmprasād's poems function at psychic levels you can't approach or recover through "grown-up" emotions. Their greatest effect comes when you, the listener, are shorn like him to a naked, raw exposure.

: Bhānusiṃha (Rabindranath Tagore)

(1861—1941)

1

Spring at last! The amuyās flare,
half-opened, trembling with bees.
A river of shadow flows through the grove.
I'm thrilled, dear trusted friend,
shocked by this pleasure-flame—
am I not a flame in his eyes?
His absence tears at me—
love blooms, and then spring
blows the petals from the world.
In my heart's grove the cuckoos pour out
a bewildering fountain of pleasure-drops,
jewels of the universe.
Even the bee-opened flowers mock me:
"Where's your lover, Rādhā?
Does he sleep without you
on this scented night of spring?"

> I know he breathes secrets to you—
> I can see their perfumes still dispersing
> among the leaves of your longing.
> Have I no memory of my own?
> Besides, your head is full of flowers.
> Go wait for him in the last shreds

of your innocence, crazy girl,
until grief comes for you.

:CT & TKS

3

He never came to me.
In the whole long dark he never came
to tend my lacerated heart.
I'm a girl with nothing, a tree
with neither flowers nor fruit.

> Go home, poor tragedy. Distract yourself
> with chores, dry your eyes. Go on now,
> dear tattered garland, limp with shame.

How can I bear this staggering weight?
I'm budding and blooming at once,
and dying, too, crushed by thirst
and the leaves' incessant rustling.
I need his eyes in mine, their altar's gold fire.
Don't lie to me. I'm lost in that blaze.
My heart waits, fierce and alone.
He'll leave me. If he leaves me, I'll poison myself.

> He drinks at love's fountain, too,
> my friend. His own thirst will call him.
> Listen to Bhānu: a man's love
> whets itself on absence if it's true.

:CT & TKS

BHĀNUSIṂHA (RABINDRANATH TAGORE)   [253]

Your flute plays the exact notes of my pain.
It toys with me.
Where did you learn such stealth,
such subtle wounding, Kān?
The arrows in my breast
burn even in rain and wind.
Wasted moments pulse around me,
wishes and desires, departing happiness—
Master, my soul scorches.
I think you can see its heat in my eyes,
its intensity and cruelty. So let me drown
in the cool and consuming Yamunā,
or slake my desire in your cool,
consoling, changing-moon face.
It's the face I'll see in death.
Here's my wish and pledge:
that the same moon will spill its white pollen
down through the roof of flowers
into the grove, where I'll consecrate my life
to it forever, and be its flute-breath,
the perfume that hangs upon the air,
making all the young girls melancholy.
That's my prayer.

Oh, the two of you, way out of earshot.
If you look back you'll see me, Bhānu,
warming herself at the weak embers of the past.

:CT & TKS

18

How long must I go on waiting
under the secretive awnings of the trees?
When will he call the long notes of my name
with his flute: Rādhā, Rādhā, so full of desire
that all the little cowherd-girls will start awake
and come looking for him, as I look for him.
Will he not come to me,
playing the song of Rādhā with his eyes and hands?
He will not, Yamunā.
I have one moon—Śyāma—
but a hundred Rādhās yearn for moonlight at his feet.
I'll go to the grove, companion river.
Alone, I'll honor our trysting-place.
No one will make me renounce it.

    Come with me into the dark trees.
    You'll have your tryst,
    its trembling rapture and its tears.

:CT & TKS

19

You resemble my Dark Lord Śyāma,
Death, with your red mouth
and unkempt hair, dressed in cloud.
Sheltered in your lap, my pain abates.
You are the fountain of nectar, Death,
of immortality. I say aloud
the perfect word of your name.
Mādhava has forgotten Rādhā.
But you, Dark Lord, accomplice,
you will not abandon me.
Call me now. I'll come into your arms
in tears, but soon lapse into half-closed sleep,
drowsy with bliss, my pain erased.
You won't forget me.
I hear a flute from the distant playgrounds,
the city far away—it must be yours,
for it plays my name.

Now darkness comes on, and with it a storm.
Clouds roil, and lightning slashes at the palms;
the desolate path twists into darkness.
I'm fearless now. I'll meet you there, Death,
in the old trysting-place. I know the way.

Shame on your faithlessness, Rādhā.
Death is not another name for love.
You'll learn for yourself.

:CT & TKS

21

Who wants to hear the long, miserable
story of Rādhā? Who among you
fathoms love's mystery?
The world will see my disgrace, my stains of love,
but I won't care. I'll abandon myself
for one caress from Śyāma.

I've asked you and asked you, my friends,
not to revile him, for I have risked
everything for him: my family's honor,
my friendships, my soul.
All these I pour out in sacrifice at his feet.

I know that men from the town slander
my Dark Lord's name. They know nothing of love.
If my blunt words offend you, then don't follow me
into my heart's dark trysting-place.

   Now you understand my own heart,
   which bore long ago the fire that sears you.
   Flames still flare up, in both body and mind.

:CT & TKS

22

I've fallen from my life, friend—
my tears since birth have washed my charms away.
But I've known pure love.
If I glimpse for an instant
my own Dark Lord on the forest path,
I kiss the dust at his feet a hundred times,
as if each grain were a jewel.

Unlucky, star-crossed birth.
I long to stay within the shadow
of his flute and taste from afar his dark smile.

Rādhā is the Dark Lord's Mistress!
May her pleasure be endless!

But it's grief that's endless,
a river of unseen tears.

Is your indifference endless also, Black One?
Its half-bloomed flowers fall unseen
into the river of human tears.

:CT & TKS

Bhānusiṃha (Rabindranath Tagore)

L ATE IN 1875 one of Calcutta's foremost literary journals, *Bharata,* published eight poems by a previously unheard of seventeenth-century Vaishnava poet, Bhānusiṃha. The language of the poems was Brajabuli, a Bengali literary vernacular that had gone unused for centuries. Vaishnava poets in past centuries had written in it, but the language had dropped out of use. Over the six years following those first publications, *Bharata* ran five more poems signed Bhānusiṃha. Scholars were baffled. How had a poet of such note gone unheard of until now?

Only gradually did it emerge that the poems were the discovery of a young man from a renowned, eccentric, artistic family, who claimed to have happened on the manuscript in the Calcutta library of the Brahmo Samaj. His name was Rabindranath Tagore. Tagore had been fourteen when he published the first Bhānusiṃha poems. The name Bhanu Singha (as Tagore anglicized the name in his memoirs) plays on his own name. *Bhanu* and *rabi* both mean "sun." *Singha,* lion, and *tagore* (Sanskrit: *thakkura,* landowner) each hold a secondary meaning: "chief; man of rank." These poems were, in fact, the work of a teenage poet; no Bhānusiṃha existed.

Was this a literary hoax? A biographical account of Bhānusiṃha published by Tagore in 1884 proved a biting and sardonic parody of Western scholarship. Even more, it exposed the unthinking imitation of that sort of scholasticism by Indian scholars, full of stiff hyperbole and unproven assumptions backed by obscure books, and both slavish and arrogant in manner.

Several worlds meet in these poems. There is the Eastern Indian and Bengali tradition of song cycles dedicated to the loves of Radha and Krishna, a heritage begun by Jayadeva in the twelfth century, adopted by Vidyāpati, Chandidāsa, and other vernacular poets from the fifteenth century forward. But the Bhānusiṃha poems are also the earnest, possibly angry and rebellious, youthful work of India's pre-eminent modernist poet, who had spearheaded the Bengali Renaissance. The artists of the Renaissance were well-read and well-traveled, and likely these poems are aligned to modernist (and postmodern) practices in literary pseudonym, the elaborate Dada-style hoax, as well as early ethnopoetic projects of searching out ancient poetries (real or imaginary) as a way to rejuvenate one's own verse.

Furthermore there is the old, well-documented practice of poets assuming a persona, through possession by a god or spirit power, by being witness to supernatural events, or through receiving a vision. Which of these many possible influences worked through Tagore? His friends William Butler Yeats and Ezra Pound both revitalized their own poetry and the poetry of their day by taking on powerful personae. The tangled web of persona within persona, of seriousness within pseudonym or hoax, makes the Krishna-worshipping Bhānusiṃha lyrics both the most backward-looking and the most modern of Tagore's writing. He was still working on them at his death—which makes them the longest-standing project of his career. Could it be that what began as a hoax, meant to unseat conservative older poets and scholars, ended up the most intimate poems of Tagore's life?

: Songs of the Bengali Bauls

My life is a little oil lamp
floating on the waves.
But from which landing-pier
did you set me afloat?
With darkness ahead of me
and darkness behind,
darkness overlaps my night,
while the necklace of waves
constantly rings me about.
The storm of the night
relentlessly flows
below the stars,
and the lamp is afloat
on the shoreless water—
for company.

Gangārām

A tramp by nature and a beggar at that,
he lives a strange life, almost insane,
with values of his own which are contrary
to those of others.
His home being under a tree,
he moves from district to district
all the year round,
as a dancing beggar who owns nothing
    in the world
but a ragged patchwork quilt.

Anonymous

:DB

The scriptures will tell you
no prayers for love.
Love's record remains
unsigned by sages.

Lālan

:DB

The road to you is blocked
by temples and mosques.
I hear your call, my Lord,
but I cannot advance,
prophets and teachers
bar my way.

Since I would wish
to burn the world
with that which cools my limbs,
my devotion to unity
dies divided.

The doors of love bear many locks:
scriptures and beads.

Madan, in tears,
dies of pain and regret.

Madan

:DB

Human limbs
are held together
by a pair of lotus blooms
growing in the
lower and upper regions
of the body.
But the lotuses
open and shut
as the sun
in the body
rises and sets.

On which of these blooms
is the full moon born,
and on which the darkest
night of the month?

On which of these lotuses
rests the total eclipse
of the sun
and the moon?

Chandidās Gosāiñ

:DB

Now is the time for you
to repeat the names
of Rādhā and Krishna,
the gods of devoted love.

The central beam
of your life is down
and your time is gone.
Your cheeks are sunk
and your hair is slack,
dead as a mop of jute.
Now is the time to repeat
the names of Rādhā and Krishna.

A fading rainbow,
you balance on a stick,
bent as a letter of the alphabet,
knees and head together.
Your time has gone
and all for nothing.
Your teeth are missing
but your eyes,
through empty holes,
still frown from your brows.

Rāmachandra

:DB

Prepare your heart
day by day
till it is ready
for the rise of the full moon.
Then lay a trap
at the bottom of the river
to catch it.

Pulin

:DB

Bauls of Bengal

"God's vagabonds," they've been called, and they'll refer to themselves as "madmen." Their madness is social, not medical; it stems from a sure-footed disregard of civic or religious convention. Caste they fiercely reject, and contempt they level at the scripture-based religion most Bengalis follow. Though regarded as wanderers, troubadors, street beggars, and vagabonds, the Bauls of Bengal generally live in small farming communities, devoted to a guru living or buried in the near vicinity. Mostly rural, drawn from laboring castes, their beliefs put them at odds with conventional Bengali lifestyle. The most celebrated of Bauls, Lālan (circa 1774—1890), once sang:

> What form does caste take?
> Brother, I've never seen it
> not with these eyes.
> (DB translation)

Scholar Kshitimohan Sen writes, "They [the Bauls] say, all these scriptures are nothing but leftovers from ancient celebrations. What are we, dogs?—that we should lick these leftovers? If there is need, we shall make new celebrations." To get what Sen says next, you need to know that *pat*, leaf, has two uses. It is the leaf of a banana or other plant used in rural areas and on train platforms for a disposable food-plate; it is also the palm leaf long used for book pages in India. "Having lost their faith, men, like dogs, collect together the left-over leaves. Even dogs one day abandon the leaves. Men are still more despicable. Their pride is in showing which among the leaves is oldest!"

The Bengali term *Baul* most likely derives from Sanskrit *vātula*—mad, insane, "affected by wind." The sect has produced hundreds of singers over the last several centuries, forty or more of them well-known. The singers perform seasonally, carrying a small stringed instrument from village to village, returning home to help bring in the harvest.

Central to Baul belief is that the presence of love is what gives spiritual stature, not observance of ritual or adherence to some creed. Love and life are joyful affairs, and religious celibacy they consider absurd. Asceticism? A dry, withered path. They reject it for a juicy (*rosik*, Sanskrit *rasika*) spirituality. Their core practice is a sexual mysticism, their beliefs drawn from aboriginal lore, the Vedas, yoga, Tantra, Krishna devotion, and Islamic mysticism. Deben Bhattacharya characterizes the way their creed takes from various sources, "discarding the system while accepting the faith." Rejection of official, organized, systematic religion—or poetry, for that matter—locates them in a worldwide underground of poets who mix mystical practice with political dissent.

Street singing is not germane to Baul spiritual life. It seems to have arisen as a way for some to earn a small livelihood, supplemented by agricultural work at home. Singers will compose their own songs or patch together lyrics learnt from others. Mostly it is the men who sing, doing so in village languages that differ a bit from district to district. Their lyrics can seem baffling, maybe because few outsiders have gotten an intimate look at their practices, and often because their songs speak in riddles—as when they call themselves madmen, or speak of the "inner man" of the heart. The charge of madness, when flung by outsiders, may show frustration or anxiety at the guarded nature of Baul religion. It's this "madness" that struck Allen Ginsberg on a visit to India in 1962–1963, along with that mix of mystical song and candid political dissent. Years later he wrote a Baul-inspired poem, "After Lalon" [Lālan]—

It's true I got caught in
the world

When I was young Blake
    tipped me off
Other teachers followed:
Better prepare for Death
Don't get entangled with
    possessions
That was when I was young,
    I was warned
Now I'm a Senior Citizen
and stuck with a million
    books
a million thoughts a million
    dollars a million
        loves
How'll I ever leave my body?
    Allen Ginsberg says, I'm
    really up shits creek

On the India trip Ginsberg met Nabani Das, a Baul who had known
Rabindranath Tagore some decades earlier. When he returned to the
States Ginsberg recommended Baul music to record producer Albert
Grossman. Keeping Ginsberg's words in mind, Grossman eventually
traveled to India, and in 1967 brought five Baul singers to New York,
housed them in a barn outside Woodstock, and introduced them to
Bob Dylan and the Band. Two of those Bauls—Purna Das and Lux-
man Das—flank Dylan on the cover of his album *John Wesley Hard-
ing*. Purna Das later stated,

> There was a great similarity between our music and his.
> There is a connection between Baul music and Western
> folk music because the subjects are nature, love, human
> bodies, sorrow, which in fact are subjects common to all
> people everywhere.

Deben Bhattacharya's translations come from field recordings he made in the 1950s traveling around Bengal, as well as from available books. They seem pretty transparent. The following poem was recorded and translated by ethnomusicologist Charles Capwell in the 1980s, for his book *The Music of the Bauls of Bengal*. More coded, it uses the automobile to transport yoga-teachings and Tantra symbolism that date back millennia. The key to Baul riddle poems, as Capwell describes some of them, may lie in ancient texts: the Upaniṣads, or farther back.

Drive the human-body-motor-car upon the road of *sadhona*.*
Be informed of who is your mind-driver
    by the word of a true guru.

Two lights are at the front of the car;
    they are lit night and day; they don't go out.
A car with seven locks;
        keep alert, o mind, while driving.

Within the car are two conductors;
        there are also sixteen acquitted men within.
Each is absorbed in his own work
        and has no connection with anyone.

Hiramon says, "I remember the feet of the guru;
    come and drive for me, now.
"I cannot drive your car any longer
    in this material kingdom."

Singer: Narayon Das Odhikari

---

* *sadhana*, or spiritual practice

: Coda

Wake up,
my lover of women
my amorous fluteplayer,
night has fled
it is dawn.
Shutters bang open in house after house.
Hear the bracelets
chiming together
as *gopi*s strain at their butter churns.
Wake up, it is dawn,
gods and men
throng through the doorways;
cowherding boys
their little hands stuffed with bread and butter
drive cattle to pasture.
Wake up! Mira says, wake up,
The fluteplayer will save you
but you must come
    seeking refuge.

Mirabai

: Afterword:
On Reading India's Devotional Poetry

The Spirit of Bhakti

T HE CRUCIAL TERM for most of the poetry found in this collection is *bhakti*, a Sanskrit word instantly recognizable throughout India. *Bhakti* means devotional, and refers specifically to the songs and poems of *bhaktas*, worshippers or devotees. *Bhava me bhaktaḥ*, Krishna says in the Bhagavad-gītā: "Be my bhakta."

The term derives from a verbal root, *bhaj*, which first meant to divide, share, or distribute. With time the usage came to include enjoy and participate; to eat, to make love, to adore. The notion of loving, joined with the idea of a share or distribution, came to mean something like: the portion of oneself a person gives to the spiritual or creative, or offers a deity that embodies the divine.

For North Americans the easy translation has been devotion. Bhakti poetry as devotional hymn. But in a culture still dragging Puritan attitudes into the twenty-first century, devotion carries implications of sobriety, piety, restraint, meekness; a skeptical attitude toward pleasure. At least it suggests the renunciation of reckless ecstasy.

Bhakti in India, among the singers identified with it, carries few of these qualities. Glance quickly through the tradition and you'll see that bhakti is juicy, impious, intoxicated, confrontational, often fiercely political, unremitting in how it opposes oppression. It is sexy. It delights in paradox, undermining rational thought or restraint. The nearest analogue in North America might be gospel or even the blues.

[273]

Religious, yes; devotional, at times; self-restrained, maybe. Underneath runs a current of precise disaffection. The songs are intended to establish a community of dissent—one that bases itself on love, not hierarchy, power, or prestige. Charismatic churches in North America, or revival sects based on ecstatic singing, speaking in tongues, and mystical visions, come close to the bhaktas of India.

This anyhow is what you glean from bhakti, which spread over the last 1,200 years through India—a range of spiritual and political revivals—from south to north, west to east. It is often erotic, typically anticlerical, disdainful toward piety, skeptical of scripture, hostile to ritual, incensed by social injustice. Most important for its poetry, it makes little use of logic or rationality, those tools of propriety. Extravagant, ferocious, the songs brim with irrational generosity.

I find two particular traits of bhakti poetry to highlight. The first is how much of it is pointedly, unabashedly erotic. India has excelled at love poetry for two thousand years. In fact the foremost emotional territory in the classical Sanskrit poetry that preceded bhakti was erotic love. In those poems human sexuality resonated with the erotic life of flowers, plants, birds, and mammals, all of which quicken with procreative urge in the monsoon season. The poetry considers human love calibrated to that of the natural orders. Similarly in the southern parts of subcontinent India, where Tamil stood instead of Sanskrit as the early classical language, much of the poetry turns out to be intricately romantic, placed in bioregions with specific plants and animals charging the landscapes. An ecological vision permeates the love poetry, with precise bioregional plants working to signal the arousal of erotic moods. The genius of the bhakti poets, who drew on both Sanskrit and Tamil poetry traditions, was to sweep religious and social fervor up in a wave of ecstatically charged passion. To see the entire natural world conspiring in the spiritual quest.

The theology is easy. The primary image of the soul's longing for god is given as the changing phases of love. A great deal of it revolves around the figures of Krishna and his strikingly passionate lover

Radha. In the springtime arousal of longing, the sexual rapture, the heartaches, feverish moods, jealousy, and fierce reconciliation these lovers undergo, any distinction between bodily or spiritual makes no sense. Sexual energy, flaming under the hide of every living creature—something you'll quit eating for, give up home and family for, accept social disgrace for—is the most immediate vehicle for the human spirit in its quest to shake free of ignorance and approach the divine.

The other quality of bhakti I want to point out is the razor-sharp truth-telling. The poets call out religious hypocrisy or civic injustice. They pin life and death with a cold judicious eye. Here the closest poetry in the West might be William Blake's "Auguries of Innocence," or American antiwar poems of the sixties. To read Kabir, Lal Ded, Dadu Dayal, or Janabai is to enter a world based on contraries and paradox, with only one certainty—that the stakes are the highest, and predatory behavior contains its own dreadful punishment. The poet makes his or her own life the example of the desperate need to toss into the flames every delusion, here, now, before (as Kabir says) "death grabs you by the hair."

Histories

Bhakti poetry occurs at the confluence of classical Sanskrit culture with India's many vernacular traditions. Its first emergence—the point at which scholars name the appearance of some radically new spirit—occurred in South India, in Tamil Nadu, around the eighth or ninth century. The first bhakti poems were sung in Tamil, their vision of spiritual recklessness and disdain for rigid convention drawing on pan-Indian themes. They lifted threads from Sanskrit tradition, local vernacular cultures, classical Tamil literature, the gods known to the village or city, and from movements we moderns would call political uprisings. Yet in many ways bhakti's impulse was subversive of all these. Bhakti, and the poems that convey its passions are, in translator A.K. Ramanujan's words, pointedly "anti-tradition."

That first upheaval in Tamil set many of bhakti's terms. Defiance of ritual and orthodoxy; rejection of educated speech or formal metrics; a turning away from classical training in poetry. And a search for disruptions in language that could give voice to suppressed emotion. It is remarkable how parallel bhakti's poetic discoveries sound to the innovations of the twentieth century. In imagery, rhythm, and idiom, bhakti poems show a thrust toward illogic, the use of Dada-like ruptures, distinctly personal voices pressing up through imagery that can be troubling, indecipherable, or hopelessly extravagant. A "dark, ambiguous language of ciphers," writes Ramanujan of some of the poems, and quotes historian of religion Mircea Eliade: "analogies, homologies, and double meanings."

Lest anyone think such poems simply riddles, I want to stress that behind every lyric you hear sharply articulated conflict, the struggles of a living person questioning his or her own experience in native speech. Regularly that speech manages to force new openings into language, disrupting conventional patterns of image-making or syntax. Unlike scripture or traditional religious verse—including India's classic works like the Vedas, Upaniṣads, and Bhagavad-gītā—in bhakti the poem's emotion and its drama stay focused on the poet. The poets don't sing to a distant, abstract deity, or give voice to metaphysical thought. In fact they don't bother with anything like doctrine. What they expose is a relationship. Generally this is the singer's relationship to a god or to a trickster-like teacher, rapturous, often anguished. The cries of the bhakti singers sound to me as though they come directly out of the old love poetry, with one difference. In bhakti the singer is never an observer; his or her song is not a work of art, but a vehicle driven toward freedom.

Over the course of a thousand years, measuring from eighth- or ninth-century Tamil Nadu, bhakti enveloped the south, emerged in India's western districts of Maharashtra and Gujarat, spread across the north, and eventually appeared in the eastern regions of Bengal and Orissa. A Sanskrit verse takes count of the geography.

Bhakti took birth in Dravidian lands
ripened in Karnataka, came to
womanhood in Maharashtra,
and grew crone-like in Gujarat.
Reaching Vrindavana she reemerged
a nubile young woman.
(AS translation)

This clockwise "maturation," then youthful renewal, spreading
from the south to the regions around Delhi associated with Krishna,
does not mean that bhakti was carried in a caravan region to region,
nor that it spread in some readily charted time frame. It also does
not mean—despite the Sanskrit verse—that it holds a single iden-
tity. Try to define bhakti, the paradoxes confound you at the next
bend. If religious orthodoxy takes a few standard or prescribed forms,
then the efforts to break free of social constraint are never standard,
rarely predictable. They have taken hundreds of forms in India. The
poets who come down to us look wild, untutored, sometimes quite
savage, from the standpoint of social convention. Generalize about
the poems, some hectoring poet will show up with a verse thorny
with contradiction, a swift image that tangles your feet, a phrase that
dumps logic into the Godavari River.

What Is a Bhakti Poem?

Bhakti poetry begins with the human voice. Its poems are to be
sung, danced, recited, chanted. The late Dilip Chitre, a celebrated
Indian poet who translated several volumes of the Varkari tradition
of Maharashtra into English, applies a serviceable term, *orature*. In
almost every instance bhakti is oral poetry—orature, not literature,
spoken by the poet, transcribed to the page later. In many cases centu-
ries later. In this sense its natural habitat originally was, and remains,
performance.

This means that a translation, printed on the page, will generally show only part of what the poem is: the linguistic elements. And of those, largely the elements that seem to be "meaningful." Translation cannot replicate tones of speech, the steep climbs and ornamental descents of the singer's voice, the insistent repetition of words and phrases. It cannot readily convey vocal sounds that hold no fixed meanings, or rework words that undergo deliberate or ritual distortion. Here is where translators have had to find echoes in our written language, parallels that echo what the early poets achieved. Or they've had to simply work from the page and forgo much that was carried outside the "words" of the poem.

The widespread presence of subterranean and folk traditions through India, magical or mystical in nature, should alert us to the possibility that the most important part of a song may not be "what it says." Magical language-use occurs among most tribal and nonliterate people. Traditions such as yoga and Tantra cultivate the paradox, the cipher, the surrealist or dream technique. They sometimes invent initiatory or secret languages-within-language. Some of the bhakti poets were trained in these darker corridors of *ulaṭbāṃsī* "upside-down speech" (a term used of Kabir's poetry), though these many years distant from Lal Ded or Rāmprasād Sen it proves impossible to untangle the stories about their lives and say with certainty what training they had.

In this context I need to point out that over the last hundred years bhakti has become comfortably situated in India's religious traditions. Prior to that it existed apart from centers of power. Reading poetry that holds a spiritual charge, we need to remain alert to how the old songs may have been distorted or corrupted over the centuries to serve the ends of sectarian religion, ethnic exclusion, or nationalism. Oral poetries have no state to protect them and no high technology (such as writing, a powerful technology) to solidify or render them incorruptible. They remain vulnerable—not just to change, which is their living condition as they pass through the years—but to appropriation.

Certainly tales and popular stories of the lives of many bhakti poets seem built up in layers. Priests and scholars have taken low-caste or outcaste poets and "brahmanized" them: provided them fabulous births to cloud their marginal origins, named a properly orthodox guru, identified a husband they submitted to, or forged other distortions that brought poets in out of the cold and dressed them for church. If the life stories underwent this kind of pressure at times, how can we doubt that some songs got twisted to fit someone's agenda? Later assimilation to powerful creeds, recognition of individual poets by kings or emperors, or the development of sectarian groups around dead poets can leave modern readers with a skewed sense of what that poet meant during his or her own day.

The Six Roads of Bhakti Poetry

Because this is an anthology of printed material, most of it oral to start with, often passed along through song for centuries, I am going to draw up some characteristics of the bhakti poem worth keeping in mind. The greatest change, the biggest effect of translation, might not have occurred when the poem crossed from Hindi or Bengali to English. It may have come years earlier, when a song performed on the street was transformed into a written text, congealed in ink or type-font, made invariable. Writing is "the solid form of language" (Robert Bringhurst).

I've reworked some features of oral poetry pointed out by American poet Jerome Rothenberg in his 1968 collection, *Technicians of the Sacred: A Range of Poetries from Africa, America, Asia, Europe & Oceania*. Rothenberg wanted to show points of contact between "primitive poetry" and twentieth-century avant-garde texts. He provided contemporary poets with a raw sense of how the preliterate past stands hand in hand with the present. Drawing on Rothenberg's thoughts, I've drawn up six features that characterize the bhakti poem. I call them roads.

1. The poem is carried by the poet's voice. It has been composed orally, often spontaneously. Only later has someone written it down. Frequently its model or source of inspiration was local folk tradition. The full range of the vocal might be employed, along with instrumental music. The poem is recited, intoned, sung, chanted. No two presentations will sound the same. Reading a bhakti poem, keep the drum skin close to hand.

2. The poem uses a highly developed process of thinking in images. Often these images are held tense by conflict, or built out of polarity. The order of images or "lines" would not necessarily have been fixed. Contradiction, illogic, paradox, noncausal thought—the poet puts these to use. Narrative comes in bright, sharp images and personal cries, not plot or storytelling. Even emotions won't stay consistent. Walt Whitman's "Do I contradict myself? Very well then . . . . I contradict myself," would be familiar to the *bhakta*. Images may owe their logic to dream, trance, linguistic puzzle, the supernatural, the "weird."

3. Meaning emerges in the poet's fierce involvement—a minimal art of maximum involvement, or "intensity." Hence the poem is romantic, not classical. The poem transfers energy through the poet's white-hot contact with reality, not through rules of composition or skilled working of known themes. Honesty over eloquence. The words can sound rough, slangy, uncooked.

4. These are public events, taking place among listeners or spectators. The poet creates a theater of participants. The poem pulls the listener into its world—even the unwilling. This "world" is not a figure of speech; it is an alternative society, governed by

love, not law. Hectoring, vows and oaths, confrontational prod-
ding, are not to make enemies but to draw the reluctant into
relationship with the poet's alternative world. There are warn-
ings, pleas, curses, outcries. Questions rather than answers. The
poet sings a counterculture into existence, a community that
would live by the urgency of the poem.

5. The poem is an act of body—animal-body-rootedness—as
   much as spirit. It calls attention to their inseparability: body-
   and-spirit. Dance, a potent "technique of ecstasy," is frequently
   central to the performance, along with the mammal range of
   vocal sounds: growls, sighs, purrs, weeping. Sexuality can get
   channeled through the poem; it raises the body to a state of
   heightened alertness.

6. The poet-as-shaman controls the "techniques of ecstasy" (Mir-
   cea Eliade's term). A song uses every available figure of language
   to reach insight or vision, and to transmit that vision to a lis-
   tener. This means the poem is neither didactic nor descriptive.
   Its aim is to project the listener into other "states." It sancti-
   fies the participants and their landscape: time and space made
   sacred.

Nirguna or Saguna

The standard distinction in scholarly and theological accounts of
bhakti is worth mentioning. It takes stock of whether the poet sings
to a personal deity that has not only a name but a definite form: a
birth, a collection of deeds and stories, a geographic location. This is
saguna, sa-guna, with-attributes. Figurative.

The contrary mode is one in which the poet finds any description
of spiritual reality limited. Gods are impermanent, thus no point
of refuge. Worse, a god may be an illusion, a projection of personal

fear, desire, or self-satisfaction, rather than a true assertion about the personality of the universe. Hence *nirguna*, free of attributes. Nonfigurative.

Sometimes the *nirguna / saguna* distinction breaks down. Certain poets—Lal Ded, Kabir, the Bauls—come to us with poems in both modes.

The major *saguna* deities fall loosely into three forms: Vishnu, Śiva, and, particularly in India's eastern states, the Goddess (Śakti). When you look closely, though, since bhakti emerged from and remains close to vernacular traditions, trying to disentangle any number of deities seems nearly fruitless. If you have traveled rural India, even in modern times, or burrowed into some urban neighborhood, keeping straight the countless gods and goddesses that come and go from the fields, linger at a pool of water, or lie sheltered in a tree root, rock grotto, or fuse box, is daunting. That task is best left to the experts. In Maharashtra a name for Vishnu may carry attributes identified elsewhere with Śiva. In Bengal, the various goddesses, Kālī, Durgā, Pārvatī, and Umā, shift into one another; nobody finds this weird. Sometimes big names get laid over local names. Sometimes nobody knows where the local names came from.

Krishna is pan-Indian, though, and accounts of his life, particularly his love affair with the cowherd girl Radha, lie at the heart of a great deal of the poetry in this volume. I can't explain why this story grips the bhakti poets again and again. Historians surmise that Krishna is an indigenous deity, not an "import" brought to India by the Indo-Aryan settlers who entered and took possession of much of the South Asian subcontinent four thousand years ago. In bhakti, Krishna's preferred form is a mischievous, irresistible, almost unwittingly seductive teenager, thin as a willow switch, his skin glistening blue-black or raven-dark.

Krishna carries and plays the "seven musical notes" of the nomad's flute, an instrument common since the last ice age. Hearing it the village women of Vrindavana district go crazy with desire. They slip out of their houses at night—abandoning the settled, agrarian life with its round of chores, servitude to the calendar, endless concern about rainfall, and abandonment of ecstasy. All this they leave behind, to dance and make love with Krishna in the groves of the dark-barked, white-blossomed tamala trees (*Cinnamomum tamala*). These cow-herd girls are the *gopi*s; among them is one, Radha, who over time becomes Krishna's favorite. The poets sing mostly of her. It is the mystical consummation of love between Krishna and Radha that lies at the heart of so much Vaishnava bhakti poetry. The poet, even the male poet, will adopt the role of Radha. (Are not all souls female before god, asked Mirabai, when a priest tried to exclude her from a temple complex because she was a woman.)

Krishna goes by many names. Mirabai calls him Śyām (Dark One), as does Surdās; Mirabai also calls him Giridhara, "the Energy that lifts mountains," in Robert Bly's phrase. Other poets sing to Govinda, Keśava, Pitāmbara, Hari, Mādhava, referring to his cowherd life, his hair, his saffron-colored clothes, his honeyed sweetness. Those who approach him through song or poetry believe that we live in a dark era, the Kali Yuga, a period of ruin and spiritual confusion. Only by harnessing the most elemental energy of the spirit—the love that animates our glands—can we humans survive. To use this inner force to approach the energy that lifts mountains.

The Context

For North Americans I would like to say that the poets in this book edge close to the erotic mysticism of Walt Whitman's "Song of Myself." But few were able to share Whitman's peculiarly modern optimism, which stemmed from the raw newness of American society and his excitement over democracy. India's poets have faced an ancient, deeply entrenched culture, which over time developed a frighteningly rigid caste system, a dependence on the authority of priests, and painful inequality between the sexes.

Many of the poets emerged from dispossessed orders of society: servants, shoemakers, cotton carders, sweepers, collectors of refuse, as well as women, orphans, and religious outcasts. Even those who did not arise from low stature—the Brahmans among them—infuriated the orthodox by singing or writing in vernacular languages, rather than Sanskrit, the priest's tongue that excluded women and the low castes. In Chandidāsa's case, persecution came because as a temple priest he carried on a public, all-consuming love affair with a village washerwoman. In response he cried, "I throw ashes at all laws / Made by man or god."

Despite the way many were persecuted, or more likely because of it, the poets of bhakti seem to walk instinctively toward Whitman's dream of equality. And don't overlook what fine poets many were. Kabir and Mirabai are deservedly known in the West, through books and concert recitations; many others deserve modern readers. To North Americans, this tradition, bhakti, does not look like an argument in India's religious systems. It is a living tradition of the brave and rebellious, forcing innovations in speech as a way of changing their world.

During worldwide political upheavals in the 1960s American poet Kenneth Rexroth defined the "counterculture" as "people who live by the tenets of lyric poetry." This rings true for the poets of medieval India. What sets them apart from their classical Sanskrit or Tamil predecessors—making them a significant cultural force—is their resolve to match life and poetry. To live by what they sing no matter the consequences. If the stories are true, several bhakti poets gathered "communities of dissent" around themselves in their lifetimes. Others were hounded, mocked, beaten, exiled. They drew from the storehouse of Indian myth, poetics, music, and imagery, but the passions they sang were designed to shatter any manacles of thought that would limit the bright heat of experience.

Deben Bhattacharya (1921—2001) was a musicologist, film-maker, and writer renowned in particular for his field recordings. His translations from Bengali poets and singers into English were for many years the most influential volumes available. He made record-ings throughout Bengal, bringing the classical and folk music of India to England and the United States. Bhattacharya divided his time between Calcutta and Paris until his death in 2001.

Robert Bly, born in 1926 in the state of Minnesota, has been a controversial poet and counterculture leader since 1966 when he founded American Writers against the Vietnam War. Through the 1950s, '60s, and '70s he edited poetry journals committed to trans-lation and an internationalist view of literature. Bly remains one of North America's most visible poets and translators.

Dilip Chitre (1938—2009) was one of the foremost writers and critics of post-Independence India. He wrote in both Marathi and English, and translated extensively from the Varkari tradition—nota-bly the complete poems of Tukaram in three volumes. Also a painter and filmmaker, Chitre helped found the journal *Shabda* in 1954, and served as honorary editor of the journal *New Quest* until his death in 2009.

Ananda Coomaraswamy (1877—1947), born in Colombo, Sri Lanka, moved to England as a young man. His many writings on Indian art, philosophy, metaphysics, poetry, and music were among the first serious studies available to the West. After relocating to the

United States in 1917 he moved in avant-garde circles in New York and Boston. Coomaraswamy served as keeper of Indian art at the Boston Museum of Fine Arts; much of this first permanent collection of South Asian art in North America was developed out of his own personal collection.

VIDYA DEHEJIA is an art historian and curator. With training in Tamil and Sanskrit, as well as several modern Indian languages, she serves as a professor of Indian art at Columbia University. Her publications and exhibits range in content from early Buddhist art to Chola dynasty bronzes to photography.

EDWARD C. DIMOCK JR. (1930—2001) was professor emeritus in South Asian languages and literatures at the University of Chicago. He traveled to Calcutta in 1955 and is remembered as a father figure to the generation of American scholars who studied in India after World War II. Dimock wrote and translated extensively from the Bengali. In 1992, the Indian government awarded Dimock its highest honorary degree, Desikottama, for lifetime achievement.

KALI MOHAN GHOSE (1884—1940) was a cofounder of the London Brahmo Samaj in 1912, along with Rabindranath Tagore and William Rothenstein. In London he met the American poet Ezra Pound, and their Kabir translations helped introduce the great *bhakta* poet to England. Ghose later became a lawyer of the Kolkata High Court.

HANK HEIFETZ is an independent American poet, student of Sanskrit, and translator, who collaborates with South Asian scholars on volumes of early Indian poetry. He has published translations of Kālidāsa's *Kumārasambhava*, Tamil songs of war and wisdom with George Hart, and versions of Dhūrjaṭi with Velcheru Narayana Rao.

LINDA HESS, born in 1941, is a Zen student and an associate professor of religious studies at Stanford University. Her work on Kabir is featured in a recent film from the Kabir Project, a series of films, recordings, books, and performances undertaken by filmmaker Shabnam Virmani (www.kabirproject.org).

JANE HIRSHFIELD, born in 1953, is a poet, translator, essayist, and editor. She has been closely associated with Buddhist communities in California and cotranslated *Ink Dark Moon: Poems by Ono no Komachi and Izumi Shikibu* with Mariko Aratani. Her books include the recent poetry volume *Come, Thief,* as well as *Women in Praise of the Sacred: Forty-Three Centuries of Spiritual Poetry by Women.*

ARUN KOLATKAR (1931—2004) was one of India's finest modern poets. He wrote prolifically in both Marathi and English. Hesitant about publishing his work, he did not release a book until the age of forty-four, when *Jejuri* came out and won the Commonwealth Poetry Prize. His *Collected Poems in English* (Bloodaxe Books), which includes his translations of Varkari poets, came out in 2010, edited and with a long biographical introduction by his friend Arvind Krishna Mehrotra.

DENISE LEVERTOV (1923—1997) was born and published her first poetry in England. In 1948 she relocated to the United States, becoming one of the preeminent members of "the new American poets," the post-World War II generation of experimentalists. Levertov was a staunch antiwar activist. Her commitment to "organic form" in poetry—rather than the use of received forms—remains influential. Her best-known titles appeared during the Vietnam War, including *Life in the Forest* and *Relearning the Alphabet.*

J. MOUSSAIEFF MASSON (now publishing as Jeffrey Masson), born in 1941, is an independent scholar and author. He studied, taught, and translated Sanskrit poetry and important works of Sanskrit poetics before leaving academic life to pursue controversial and groundbreaking work on Freud and psychoanalysis.

ARVIND KRISHNA MEHROTRA, born in 1947 in Lahore, is a renowned poet, editor, and translator. His *Songs of Kabir* was published in the US by NYRB Classics in 2011. He is the author of four books of poetry, edited the collected poems of his friend Arun Kolatkar, and divides his time between Mumbai and Dehradun.

W.S. MERWIN, born in 1927, has published fifty books of poetry. These include translations from Spanish, French, Italian, and Middle English, as well as several Asian languages. Buddhist practice and deep ecology have been active concerns in his poetry for several decades, and he lives in Hawaii where he works on preservation and restoration of the rain forests. From 2010 to 2011 he served as Poet Laureate of the United States.

LEONARD NATHAN (1924—2007) was a poet, critic, and professor of rhetoric at the University of California, Berkeley. He collaborated on translations from many languages, notably with the Nobel Prize-winning Polish poet Czesław Miłosz. He studied Sanskrit and produced a fine edition of Kālidāsa's *Meghadūta*.

GIEVE PATEL, born in 1940, is a consequential presence in modern Indian poetry. A doctor by profession, he is also known as a playwright and painter. He has published three books of poetry (*Poems*; *How Do You Withstand, Body*; and *Mirrored Mirroring*); published three plays (*Princes*; *Savaksa*; and *Mister Behram*); and held exhibitions of his paintings in India and abroad. He lives in Mumbai.

EZRA POUND (1885—1972), one of America's leading modernist innovators, argued in his polemical essays for an international approach to literature. Among his many translations are the medieval troubadors of Provence, Tang dynasty Chinese poets, and the classic anthology of Confucius. His monumental poem *The Cantos* was a fifty-year project, still the most influential English-language modernist epic, and is credited with expanding the range of poetry in unprecedented ways.

A.K. Ramanujan (1929—1993) was a poet, essayist, and translator from the languages of South India. He has been honored with a volume in the Oxford India series. Among his translations are *Speaking of Śiva*, two volumes of poetry by Nammalvar, and a collection of classical Tamil verse, *Poems of Love and War*. He taught for many years at the University of Chicago.

Velcheru Narayana Rao taught Telugu and Indian literatures for thirty-eight years at the University of Wisconsin, Madison. He also taught at the University of Chicago, and is currently visiting distinguished professor of South Asian studies at Emory. He has published fifteen books including *Twentieth Century Telugu Poetry*, and has collaborated closely with American poets and scholars on translations of South Indian poetry.

Andrew Schelling, born in 1953, has published six volumes of poetry from Sanskrit and other languages of India, as well as a dozen books of his own poetry and essays. *Dropping the Bow: Poems from Ancient India* received the Academy of American Poets translation award in 1992. Other titles include *From the Arapaho Songbook* and *The Real People of Wind and Rain*. He teaches poetry and bioregional writing at Naropa University, serves on the arts faculty at Deer Park Institute in India's Himalayan foothills, and has worked with the Public School, an outgrowth of Occupy Oakland.

Clinton Seely, born in 1941, is a scholar of Bengali language and literature. He studied at the University of Chicago and for his PhD dissertation wrote a biography of Jibanananda Das. Among writers he has translated are Rāmprasād Sen, Buddhadeva Bhose, and Michael Madhusudan Dutt. Seeley also designs software for the Bengali language.

SHUKDEO SINGH is a retired professor of Hindi at Banaras Hindu University.

GARY SNYDER, born in 1930, is author of nearly twenty collections of poetry and prose. For decades he has been outspoken as one of North America's influential thinkers and activists on wilderness, ecology, land use, and environmental concerns. In 1975 he received the Pulitzer Prize for *Turtle Island*, and his readings, lectures, and performances with musicians have set the tone for an ecological and internationalist approach to poetry in North America as well as Japan and Europe.

TONY K. STEWART, born in 1954, is a Bengali religion and literature specialist, currently Gertrude Conaway Vanderbilt Chair in Humanities at Vanderbilt University. In collaboration with Edward C. Dimock Jr. he published a translation of the Bengali and Sanskrit hagiographies of Caitanya, entitled *Caitanya Caritāmṛta of Kṛṣṇadāsa Kavirāja* (Harvard Oriental Series, 1999).

CHASE TWICHELL, born in 1950 in New Haven, Connecticut, has lived for many years in the Adirondack Mountains of upper New York State. She has published numerous collections of poetry, and her work frequently reflects her commitment to Buddhist insight. She left a career of teaching behind, to found Ausable Press, an enterprise dedicated to publishing poetry.

From *The Kabir Book* by Robert Bly. Copyright © 1971, 1977 by Robert Bly. Copyright © 1977 by the Seventies Press. Reprinted by permission of Beacon Press, Boston.

Mirabai, translated by Andrew Schelling. From *For Love of the Dark One: Songs of Mirabai*, Hohm Press. Copyright © 1993, 1998 by Andrew Schelling. Reprinted by permission of Hohm Press.

From *Mirabai: Ecstatic Poems* by Robert Bly and Jane Hirshfield. Copyright © 2004 by Robert Bly and Jane Hirshfield. Reprinted by permission of Beacon Press, Boston.

Mirabai, translated by Robert Bly. From *Mirabai Versions*. Copyright © 1984 by Robert Bly. Reprinted with the permission of Ken Botnick, Red Ozier Press.

Dadu Dayal, translated by Andrew Schelling. From *Dadu*, Longhouse. Copyright © 2009 by Andrew Schelling. Reprinted by permission of Andrew Schelling and Longhouse.

Jayadeva, translated by Andrew Schelling. From *Kamini: A Cycle of Poems from Jayadeva's* Gīta-govinda, Emdash Editions. Copyright © 2007 by Andrew Schelling. Reprinted by permission of Emdash Editions.

Vidyāpati, Chandidāsa, and Govinda-dāsa, translated by Edward C. Dimock Jr. and Denise Levertov. From *In Praise of Krishna* by Edward C. Dimock and Denise Levertov, copyright © 1967 by the Asiatic Society. Used by permission of Doubleday, a division of Random House. Any third parties must apply directly to Random House for permission.

Rāmprasād Sen, translated by Leonard Nathan and Clinton Seely. From *Grace and Mercy in Her Wild Hair: Selected Poems to the Mother Goddess*, Hohm Press. Copyright © 1999 by Leonard Nathan and Clinton Seely. Reprinted by permission of Hohm Press.

"After Rāmprasād Sen" by Gary Snyder. From *The Back Country*. Copyright © 1968 by Gary Snyder. Reprinted by permission of New Directions Publishing.

Rabindranath Tagore, poems 1, 3, 10, 18, 19, 21, and 22, from *The Lover of God*, translated by Tony K. Stewart and Chase Twichell. Translation copyright © 2004 by Tony K. Stewart and Chase Twichell. Reprinted with the permission of the Permissions Company on behalf of Copper Canyon Press, www.coppercanyonpress.org.

Baul songs, translated by Deben Bhattacharya. From *The Mirror of the Sky: Songs of the Bauls of Bengal*, Hohm Press. Copyright © 1999 by Deben Bhattacharya. Reprinted by permission of Hohm Press.